MUSICAPAEDIA: La Flor de Potosí, Spanish, Beginning Level I.
ISBN: 0-9676939-4-2

12345678910

The various curricular components and pedagogical sequences in the Musicapaedia™ series of books and CDs--which use by teachers who are using their own purchased copy. Excerpts of lyrics, lessons, or form a unique approach to language learning--are, as a whole, a copyrighted and proprietary system. Duplication of this book or of the accompanying musical recordings is prohibited except for classroom musical recordings are permitted and encouraged for the purposes of reporting in the news media.

*The author of the Musicapaedia™ series implores teachers and individuals* not only to purchase their own copy, but to encourage colleagues and friends to do so as well. In this way, further such texts may be produced for your educational and aesthetic pleasure. On the website there is an offer whereby **you may receive a free book and CD of your choice if you get two of your colleagues or friends** to order any two of the three books currently available (the "3 for the price of 2" option).

**This lesson activities book is meant for use with the CD of the same name.**

**Instrumental credits for the CD:**
Tom Blodget: vocals, rhythm guitar. Mike Arntz: lead guitar on tracks 2, 3, 4, and 5. Steve Sweeney: lead guitar on tracks 1 and 6. Randy Ricks: bass on tracks 1, 3, 4, 5, and 6. Greg Punkar: bass on track 2. Rey Rodriguez: drums on tracks 2, 3, 4, and 5. Jim Toole: drums on tracks 1 and 6. Rudy Giscombe: sax on tracks 1 and 6. Gregg Dye: keyboards on tracks 1 and 6. Christopher Conrad: lead guitars, Hoffner bass, and drums on track 7. Tom Mallon: recording engineer/savior of the original 1" tape recordings to ADAT. La Flor de Potosí was produced by Tom Blodget.

**CD and bookcover design by Richard Eriksson (of San Francisco) at trikky31@yahoo.com**

**Please visit the website www.musicapaedia.com to order more copies or see and hear other Musicapaedia™ releases. <u>A complete glossary in Spanish-English for all of the exercises in this book, as well as crossword puzzles using vocabulary found in the song may be posted there for your free downloading and use.</u> Additional educational material and activities may be posted there, as well as links to sites of interest to the Spanish language learner.**

# La Flor de Potosí

## TABLE of CONTENTS

## THE SONGS: with <u>Lyrics and Learning Activities (see table p. iii)</u>

# Table of Songs and What They Teach

The seven songs on the CD head the chart below, in order of appearance. On the left-hand column descending are all of the grammatical structures and verb tenses in the songs that are also taught in exercises accompanying the song. <u>The page number where those exercises begin is given in the corresponding box.</u> Note that some grammar points are demonstrated in more than one song, so the same exercise may be indicated more than once. In a few instances the exercise that supports one of the grammar points in a song may be found in the section accompanying another song, since both songs emphasize that point. Generally, exercises related to the song immediately follow each song in the text.

| Songs:<br><br>What is taught… | 1.La Luz del Sol | 2.¿Me Quedo o Me Voy? | 3.La Fiesta | 4.Nos Gusta | 5.Amañamo | 6.Te Quiero Como Eres | 7.La Flor De Potosí |
|---|---|---|---|---|---|---|---|
| GUSTAR | p.3 | | | p.36 | | | |
| INDIRECT OBJECT PRONOUNS | | p.13 | | | | p.60 | |
| DIRECT OBJECT PRONOUNS | | | | | | p.60 | |
| -GO VERBS ('YO' FORM) | | | | | p.52 | | |
| -OY VERBS ('YO' FORM) | | p.13 | | | | | |
| SER/ESTAR | | p.10 | | | | | |
| SER W/ DESCR. ADJ | | | | | | | p.77 |
| REFLEXIVE VERBS | | p.18 | | | | | |
| RECIPROCAL REFLEXIVE VERBS | | | | | | | p.76 |
| ESTAR+PAST PARTICIPLE | | p.15 | | | | | |
| -ANDO, -IENDO GERUNDS | | | p.32 | | | | |
| DEMONSTRATIVE ADJECTIVES | | | p.28 | | | | |
| POR/PARA | | | p.30 | | | | |
| DEFINITE ARTICLES | | | | p.44 | | | |
| SABER/CONOCER | | | | | p.53 | | |
| STEM CHANGERS -IE-, -UE- and –E-to-I- | (see p.68) | | | | | p.68 | |
| PREPOSITIONAL PRONOUNS | | | | p.39 | | | |

| Songs: <br><br> What is taught… | 1.La Luz del Sol | 2.¿Me Quedo o Me Voy? | 3.La Fiesta | 4.Nos Gusta | 5.Amañamo | 6.Te Quiero Como Eres | 7.La Flor De Potosí |
|---|---|---|---|---|---|---|---|
| POSSESSIVE PRONOUNS | | | | | | p.70 | |
| *TENER QUE/ HAY QUE* | | | p.29 | | | | |
| VOCAB SEASONS | | | | | | | p.75 |
| VOCAB NATURE | p.5 | | | | | | |
| VOCAB FOOD AND DRINK | | p.26 | | | | | |
| DOUBLE OBJECT PRONOUNS | | | | | | p.66 | |
| *TAMBIEN/TAMPOCO* | | | | p.43 | | | |
| *SIN/CON* | | | | | p.56 | | |
| *CONTIGO/CONMIGO* | | | | | | p.69 | |
| *PUEDO/QUIERO/ DEBO* + INFINITIVE | | | | p.55 | | | |
| PLACEMENT OF OBJECT PRONOUNS (in present tense) | | | | | | p.63 | |
| *SIEMPRE/NUNCA;* | | | | | | p.69 | |
| *EL AGUA*➔ *LAS AGUAS* | p.4 | | | | | | |
| FRIENDLY SLANG NAMES FOR FEMALES, MALES | | | p.28 | | | | |
| *GUSTARÍA, SERÍA, QUISIERA* | | | | | | p.70 | |
| SUFFIXES: | | | | | | | |
| *-EZ* | | p.18 | | | | | |
| *-DAD* | p.5 | | | | | | |
| *-ON* | | | | p.47 | | | |
| *-SION, -CION* | | p16-17 | | | | | |
| HYPERBATON | | | | p.47 | | | |
| PROPER NOUNS and NOUNS as INDIRECT OBJECT PRONOUNS | | | | p.41 | | | |
| MASCULINE and FEMININE NOUNS | | | | p.45 | | | |

# THE IMPORTANCE OF USING THE LYRICS OF MELODIC MUSIC TO TEACH LANGUAGE ACQUISITION

*Here are some of the <u>benefits</u> of using melodic music to teach language:*

•Presenting the target language through melodic music expands yet further the **learning modality** options you are providing for your students (aural-musical).

•Probably nothing **imprints linguistic patterns better** than **words** wedded to **memorable music.** Because of the unique *impressive nature* of melodic music, students will **retain grammatical structures** and vocabulary for **the rest of their lives.**

•Students' **inherently positive response to upbeat, melodic music** makes them **completely engaged in the activity**.

•**A correlation between music** and **improved academic performance <u>*really does exist*</u>.** The currently debated question about the so-called "Mozart effect" deals only with the *passive* listening to music while studying or taking exams, which has nothing to do with the *active* learning of language through the lyrics of melodic music. Music is **mathematical** by nature, whose "terrain" provides a fertile place for language learning to take hold and develop.

•Music, being indigenous to its geographical place of creation, as well as to the cultural and social environment in which it arises, naturally transmits and reflects the **culture** in which it is created.

•Music is, of all *sounds* that exist (which is one of the *five physical senses* that we teach), *the most richly textured and interesting of sound*. The connection between "good lyrics embedded in good sound, as good literature" and *language learning*, with all of the accompanying lesson activities that are possible, is obvious.

•**Creative *culminating activities* for proficiency** take learning the language to the next level: 1) student-created booklets illustrating the lyrics, 2) karaoke, sing-along, or lip-sync video performances, 3) dramatic interpretations/mime/acting out performances, 4) dance and choreography--moving hands, head, feet, and body to the music in creative ways, and 5) re-writing the song either altogether in an original and creative lyric (for those who can), or by substituting all the nouns, or adjectives, or other parts of speech so as to make a new songlyric.

**ALL of the multiple intelligences** are addressed when teaching language through music with the appropriate accompanying exercises: linguistic, logical, social, visual, musical (of course), individual, and kinesthetic.

▶**Linguistic** because in song we deal with words, both aural and written, as well as spoken or sung by the student later on, and in extension exercises

▶**Social**, because many of the listening and doing of the exercises can be done in cooperative learning groups

▶**Visual**, for the illustrations, storyboards, or dramatic interpretation of the song

▶**Logical** because music is *by nature* mathematical and logical; and many of the Musicapaedia™ exercises run the gamut of critical thinking skills

▶**Musical**, because language is being delivered through the melodic vehicle, and also sung or lip sync-ed by the students in return

▶**Individual**, because besides homework, the exercises can always be done individually

▶**Kinesthetic**, because students can dramatically interpret, mime, choreograph, dance, act out, or percuss (stomp, clap, shake, swing, tap, sway, etc.) to a song if it so lends itself.

•Activities can (and should) be done in **cooperative learning** groups, thus promoting classroom cohesion.

•Songs and activities can be used either to **introduce** new material, or **reinforce** previously learned material.

•**MUSIC teaches LANGUAGE by way of ART. We need more beauty and art in our schools, and in our lives.** Many students today, especially in their teens, are listening to some not-so-pretty music; fortunately, in my teaching experience, those *very same students respond* to **positive** lyrics and **melodic** music!

# HOW TO USE THIS BOOK

This book is intended for teachers of Spanish in the middle, secondary or college classroom and for individuals learning on their own, or who are taking classes. Everyone will also greatly benefit from "playing and working" with the songs and lessons. Those from ages 7-70 will find exciting songs and clever lyrics herein, and challenging activities that have been designed to make learning Spanish a delightful and satisfying experience.

The Musicapaedia™ lesson books and musical CDs may be the most effective and enjoyable off-the-shelf supplementary classroom resources that a world language teacher may *ever use* in his or her teaching career, or that an individual may embrace while otherwise struggling to learn the language in a more formal setting or bravely on one's own. (At least that's my biased opinion based on my experience!)

## Supplementary reference books recommended
Those who use this book and CD can profit *without* the aid of a formal text, since much of the necessary grammatical explanations are provided; but this does not contain the complete information that a formal text for beginning students would have. Ideally, this book and CD should supplement a systematic language course with a standard text as a reference, as some basic knowledge about Spanish is assumed (subject pronouns, how to conjugate a verb in person and number, indefinite articles, etc.). Most students will find a good dictionary helpful, as well as verb and grammar books for reference. Below are my recommendations. The publishers of these texts are not aware I'm recommending them; they are simply what I consider to be the most useful books for those who really want to learn the language:

*Oxford Spanish-English Dictionary*, as close to unabridged as possible. The nearly unabridged version is about 33% off the $45 list price at EdwardRHamilton.com or from any comprehensive bookstore. I have found this dictionary to be the most incisive and copious with its examples.

*English Grammar for Students of Spanish*, Emily Spinelli, The Olivia and Hill Press, (734) 663-0235. By explaining both the basics of Spanish and English grammar, students' confusion is greatly cleared up. It's a slim and easy-to-digest little book at around $10.

*1001 Pitfalls in Spanish*, Third Edition, Marion P. Holt and Julianne Dueber, Barron's Educational Series, Inc., $10.95. Barron's has many other excellent books with writing activities for beginning Spanish.

*501 Spanish Verbs*, Christopher Kendris, Barron's Educational Series, used copies abound.

## To Reinforce or Introduce New Material
The Musicapaedia™ songs can be used either to *introduce* or to *reinforce* the theme, function, grammar, or verb tense you are teaching.

## What Level?

This book and musical CD, along with *¡Hola Mi Amigo!* (1999), are both for the beginning level and form the first two of a projected three books and CDs for the beginning level in this Musicapaedia™ series. If you enjoy this book and CD, please order *¡Hola Mi Amigo!* online at www.musicapaedia.com. If you are ready to go to the next level, purchase *La Feria de Abril*, which has 8 songs and lessons for both the intermediate and advanced levels.

## Types of activities and exercises

Many of the exercises that accompany a Musicapaedia™ song draw from unavoidably standard methods of stimulating responses from the learner, such as cloze listening exercises, fill-in-the-blank, matching, crosswords, multiple choice, completion, open-ended answers, and so on. These are all very useful means to stimulate cognition and draw out responses from the would-be learner who has been exposed to the song. The signature and hallmark of the Musicapaedia™ series of songs and lessons is not only the optimal use of these long-valid devices, but a combination of others in addition, such as the following:

1.  A "cloze" exercise of missing lyrics (or even just the vowels--see *¡Hola Mi Amigo!*);
2.  Extension exercises of grammatical points highlighted by the song;
3.  Most Musicapaedia™ songs can be illustrated, story-boarded, mimed, dramatized, or filmed;
4.  Songs have a set of "short answer" oral questions to ask students after hearing the song several times, to check for comprehension;
5.  Pattern recognition. Learners are given a variety of target words/phrases to mark during listening, such as gender-based nouns, verb conjugations according to person or number, theme vocabulary words, etc;
6.  Exercises that emphasize "critical thinking", at all levels of Bloom's Taxonomy.
7.  Students familiarize themselves with the vocabulary by having the English translation of the song in a column list, in order of appearance in the song, listed either by single words but usually by meaningful phrases, and students compare this list with the song itself, and must write the Spanish next to the English, having to decide on each line where the break is. This allows students to learn the word without having to "look it up", because the known words or phrases immediately before and after an unknown word or phrase isolates it, and it must mean what the translation at the right indicates. This Musicapaedia™ method of vocabulary-building is, challenging, effective, and a breakthrough in language teaching.

Many of the songs have a "love interest" (the lyrics are very tame by today's standards) that is universally appealing, and moreover, they lend themselves to classical literary interpretation. Having been exposed by my studies in literature, both in English and in Spanish, to literary concepts in prose and in poetry, I have done my best to apply them in the songwriting and in many of the exercises. Some of these activities are challenging, and if not done as homework, are best done in pairs or groups.

## Culminating Activities

So as to offer to students in your class the opportunity to express themselves in ways beyond the orthodox curriculum, the Musicapaedia™ songs lend themselves to:

Ámusic video (see below for how easy this is to do*)

Ástoryboard/booklet illustration with lyrics

Álip sync or karaoke voice-over (instrumental version is provided for each song)

Áa capella or prose/poem recitation of the lyrics from memory

Ástudent learning and playing the song on their own instrument

ÁPowerpoint™ or other computer software illustration of the song with lyrics scrolling

Ádramatic interpretation or mime

Áchoreography/dance

Áre-writing one's own lyrics, or a variation of the original, to perform with the instrumental track provided

I have witnessed many performances and works by students in most of the above activities in my own classes over the years. It is a wonderful opportunity to let art bloom in the classroom, and to combine learning with fun and class cohesion.

*The way to make the video is quite simple. Here are the steps:

1) Analyze the lyrics and decide where the "scene breaks" are. Mark them on the lyric sheet.

2) Play the song, and using a timing watch, mark at what second the scene needs to "break" (it really doesn't matter if you're off by a second).

3) Decide who is going to participate in the filming and acting, and go shoot the scenes. In the camera, at the beginning of shooting, set the timer to 0:00. If the first scene is 7 seconds long, film it and stop at 0:07. Shoot the next scene, and so on. If you make a mistake and film too long, just rewind and film it again until you get the action to end at the right time. You can talk to your actors at the same time because you are basically doing a "silent film" and will add the musical soundtrack later, or just play a boombox and turn the conversational sound off of the video when playing it for the class.

4) When done filming, add the soundtrack to the audio of the film itself, if you know how, or have the facility. The poor man's way of doing it is to just practice the timing of the beginning of the song with the film, so that the film plays along with the song. In a couple of takes, you can decide that the song (or the film) is to start first, at a certain signal point; you press the buttons to the CD player and the video at the remembered time, and amazingly, if you had good actors and production, the video will almost seem professional!

**Cooperative Learning (though not absolutely necessary) is highly recommended.**
The Musicapaedia™ lessons vary from the mechanically simple to the intellectually challenging, and everything in between. Please don't overlook the wonderful possibility that--in **cooperative learning groups**--students can profit from *every exercise* (*Cooperation in the Classroom*, Johnson, et al, tel. 612.831.9500). When there are 2-4 students together, working toward a common end, perhaps in a game format, a friendly "group competition," or even without any extrinsic rewards at all, working socially, exercises that seem difficult at first melt away before the powerful energies of cooperative learning.

# 10-Step Lesson Plan for each Musicapaedia™ Song

The lesson activities that accompany Musicapaedia™ songs highlight and exercise every learning point possible from the song's lyrics. For students to interact meaningfully with the songs, a proven lesson sequence has been designed that takes fullest advantage of the thematic, grammatical, and cultural qualities of the song. Here is the Musicapaedia™ 10-step lesson plan:

1. (4 minutes) Play the song--students write on binder paper all the **words they recognize**

2. (1 minute) Hand out **"cloze" lyric sheet** (either missing words or missing vowels)

3. (7 minutes) Play the song (at least twice)--**students fill in blanks from Word Bank** (or don't use word bank if students can handle the level)

4. (4 minutes) Play the song--students circle or underline **predetermined grammar or vocabulary targets** (all verbs conjugated "yo", clothing, etc.)

5. (2 minutes) **Review** correct answers

6. (10 minutes) **Oral questions**, mostly yes/no, either or, or short answer; teacher to student.

7. (20 minutes, but very important) Do English-to-Spanish **vocabulary list. Students write the Spanish** next to the English, which is in the order of appearance in the song, yet sometimes by phrases instead of words. (This is faster and more interesting for the student to do than looking up words in the dictionary.)

8. (2 minutes) Hand out **written exercises**.

9. (30-75 minutes) Now that students have all the knowledge and practice they need so as to succeed in the written exercises, they may **work in pairs** to finish, or assign as homework.

10. (Homework, 1-10 hours) **Culminating activities**. Finally, students can memorize the song to sing with karaoke tracks (provided), memorize only the lyrics for recital, illustrate the song, create a Powerpoint™ presentation, do a "music video," learn the song on an instrument and sing and play it, etc.

Order through the website
**http://www.musicapaedia.com**

## 1. La Luz del Sol

<u>Idiomatic expressions to know before hearing the song:</u>
*a pesar de--in spite of*
*en voz alta--out loud*
*así que--so, therefore*
*el más allá--the great beyond*

—

El _____ amanece
Aunque ya es de _____
El alba aparece
Y la luz del _____ nos va a saludar

En el _____ los del pueblo cultivamos la hortaliza
Nos _____ mucho, no nos falta
Cosechamos mucho a pesar de la pedriza
Así _____ canto en voz alta:

—

Si te orientas al viejo sol, el eternal
Despiertas la divinidad
Si penetras en el _____ de la luz universal
Encuentras la infinidad

—

El _____ amanece
Aunque ya es de _____
El alba aparece
Y la luz del _____ nos va a saludar

Celebramos el poder que en el alma _____
Por la _____ más estrecha entro
Existe la verdad y la belleza _____ allá
El _____ allá que está dentro

copyright Tom Blodget 1979 and February 18, 2003

## El Banco de Palabras:
These are the words that are missing in the song:

campo   centro   día   está   gusta   más   noche   puerta   que   sol

# Vocabulario

Below are the words and phrases of the song in English, in the order of their appearance in the song. Fill in quickly as much of the Spanish as you know, without looking up any words in the dictionary or glossary. Any words or phrases that you *don't* know, which are "sandwiched" between words you *do* know, may be confidently identified by deduction. This method eliminates the need for a dictionary.

| | |
|---|---|
| _____ | The day |
| _____ | dawns |
| _____ | although |
| _____ | now |
| _____ | it is |
| _____ | nighttime |
| _____ | The dawn |
| _____ | appears |
| _____ | and the light |
| _____ | of the sun |
| _____ | is going to greet us |
| _____ | In the country(side) |
| _____ | those |
| _____ | of the village |
| _____ | we cultivate |
| _____ | the vegetables/garden produce |
| _____ | We like it |
| _____ | a lot |
| _____ | We are not lacking (in anything) |
| _____ | We harvest |
| _____ | a lot |
| _____ | in spite of |
| _____ | the rocky soil |
| _____ | Therefore |
| _____ | I sing |
| _____ | in voice high (loud) |
| _____ | If |
| _____ | you orient yourself |
| _____ | to the |
| _____ | old |
| _____ | sun |
| _____ | the eternal |
| _____ | you awaken |
| _____ | the divinity |
| _____ | If you penetrate |
| _____ | in the center |
| _____ | of the light |
| _____ | universal |

| | you find |
| --- | --- |
| | the infinity |
| …(repeat) | |
| | We celebrate |
| | the power |
| | that |
| | in the soul |
| | is |
| | Through |
| | the door |
| | most narrow |
| | I enter |
| | Exists |
| | the truth |
| | and the beauty |
| | beyond; |
| | the beyond |
| | that is |
| | within |

## Preguntas Orales.

These questions are to check for comprehension, and should be asked orally after listening to the song several times with the above activities.

1. ¿Qué hora es, más o menos?  ¿Es por la tarde o por la mañana?

2. ¿Trabajan mucho o poco, los del pueblo?

3. ¿Qué cultivan en el campo, los del pueblo?  ¿Vegetales o peces?

4. ¿Comen bien o mal?  ¿Pasan hambre (sí o no)?

5. La tierra donde cultivan la hortaliza, ¿es de buena o mala calidad?

6. ¿Por qué "canta en voz alta" el cantante?  ¿Está feliz o triste?

7. Según el cantante, ¿dónde se encuentra la infinidad?  ¿En el centro de la luz o en la cosecha de la hortaliza?

8. Según el cantante, ¿están "la verdad y la belleza" *dentro* de la persona, o *fuera*, en el campo?

## I. Verbs that function like *gustar*

One of the seven wondrous differences between English and Spanish can be appreciated when trying to successfully learn the Spanish way of saying "I like (it)" since in Spanish it is actually equivalent to "It pleases me," which grammatically requires an English speaker to think "backwards":

| *I* | *like* | *baseball.* | | *Me* | *gusta* | *el béisbol.* |
|---|---|---|---|---|---|---|
| subject (1) | /verb (2)/ | object (3) | | object (3) | /verb (2) | /subject (1) |

There are several other common verbs that function in the same way, when used in specific circumstances. Note that in the English equivalents, the person is the *subject,* whereas the Spanish has the person as an *indirect object*, and it also comes first (!).

Spanish.                    English.

*Me falta un cuchillo.*  I need a fork *(a fork is lacking to **me**).*
*No me importa.*       I don't care *(it is not important to **me**).*
*Me gusta mucho.*     I like it a lot *(it pleases **me** a lot).*
*No nos queda mucho tiempo.*  We don't have much time *(not much time remains for **us**).*
*¿Qué te parece?*     What do you think/What is your opinion *(what does it seem to **you**)?*

**A.** All five (5) verbs are regular in the third person singular and plural (e.g. *gusta, gustan*). Choose and conjugate in the following sentences. Note that just as with *gustar,* the verb can be singular (*gusta*) or plural (*gustan*) if the subject (which usually ends the sentence in Spanish) is singular or plural:

ejemplos:
*Nos queda una hora.* There is one hour left.
*Nos quedan dos horas.* There are two hours left.

*faltar*--to lack  *importar*--to be important  *gustar*--to be pleasing to
*quedar*--time remaining  *parecer*--to seem

1. No nos ___*gustan*___ las películas (the movies)
2. ¿Te _____ los derechos (rights) humanos?
3. ¿Te _____ justo que muchas personas pasan hambre (are hungry)?
4. Nos _____ poco tiempo para remediar la situación; es muy urgente.
5. Me _____ la fuerza de voluntad (willpower).

## II. Stem-changing verbs (*despertar, encontrar, etc.*)

Please see "Te Quiero Como Eres" (song 6) for a full treatment of stem changing verbs.

## III. Feminine words that become masculine in the singular

There are two nouns in the song "La Luz del Sol" that end in -*a*, but have *el* in front of them. These words are actually feminine, and are so in the plural. The reason they don't have the word *la* in front of them is because, according to the evolutionary logic of

Spanish, the *-a* in *la* would glide indistinguishably into the *a-* at the beginning of the noun, and Spanish doesn't want that. So instead of *la agua* ("the water"), *el agua* is spoken and written. Otherwise it would have been *l'agua* or *lagua* perhaps; but it's not; it's Spanish, and they don't use contractions (except for *al* and *del*--but without a separating apostrophe). Since in the plural, the *-s* consonant makes a nice little consonantal "bump" between the two words (*la<u>s</u> almas*--the souls), no re-arrangements are needed. Note also that this exception to the rule only occurs when the spoken stress of the noun is on the first syllable (*<u>a</u>gua, <u>a</u>lma, <u>á</u>guila*, etc.). *Ambulancia*, for example, where the stress is not on the first *a-*, maintains its femininity: *La ambul<u>a</u>ncia*.

**A.** *Change the following plurals to the singular:*
1. Las aguas ➔ _____*el agua*_____ the water
2. Las águilas ➔ _____ the eagle
3. Las almas ➔ _____ the soul
4. Las albas ➔ _____ the dawn

# IV. Vocabulary of Nature.
**A.** Write the Spanish words next to the English given. They are in the order of appearance in the song.

1. _____ day
2. _____ dawns (v.)
3. _____ dawn (n.)
4. _____ night
5. _____ light
6. _____ sun
7. _____ countryside
8. _____ people/village
9. _____ we cultivate
10. _____ vegetables
11. _____ we harvest
12. _____ rocky soil
13. _____ soul
14. _____ beauty

# V. Suffixes: *-dad*

Most words in Spanish that end in *-dad* are nouns, often representing abstractions (liberty, possibility, difficulty, etc.), and can often be translated simply by changing the Spanish suffix *-dad* to the English *-ty*, and by adding or subtracting a letter or two if necessary. Sometimes the result will translate into an English word that is not in common use (*verdad* becomes *verity,* or truth); but if you know the antiquated or uncommon English word, you can figure out its modern usage.

Read the following list (aloud). You should be able to translate all of the words by substituting *-dad* with *-ty*. Note that all words ending in *-dad* in Spanish are feminine, so you may put *la* in front of each. This is not a written exercise because, with the information given, it is very easy!

Remember that in Spanish there are only five vowels, each always pronounced exactly the same. In terms of character, the following English equivalents are correct. However, native English speakers tend to draw out (or "drawl") the vowels; we tend to "ride them,"; in linguistics it's called a "glide". Pronounce "draw" slowly, and you'll notice that we say "dra-ah". A Spanish speaker would say "dra." Spanish vowels have the *qualities* or *character* as in the English examples below, but are *punchier*, more *staccato*, and are uttered in *half* the time. Keep that in mind when pronouncing the list that follows this chart:

| VOWEL | *Equivalent English sound* | *Spanish example* |
|---|---|---|
| a | like the 'a' in '**awesome**' | casa--house |
| e | like the 'a' in '**ate**' | beso--kiss |
| i | like the 'ea' in 'rep**eat**' | pito--whistle |
| o | like the 'oa' in '**boat**' | lomo--pork loin |
| u | like the 'u' in '**duty**' | luto--mourning |

*claridad, compatibilidad, credibilidad, crueldad, cualidad, dificultad, dignidad, estabilidad, eternidad, felicidad, formalidad, humanidad, legalidad, libertad, maternidad, modernidad, oportunidad, paternidad, posibilidad, probabilidad, realidad, regularidad, sexualidad, sinceridad, sociedad, solidaridad, unanimidad, unidad, utilidad, visibilidad*

**A.** The next three common Spanish words can be translated if you substitute the ending as before, but also add one more English letter to each:

1._____caridad
2._____novedad

**B.** This next list is a little harder. You may have to induce the answer from your storehouse of knowledge about more obscure English root words. First write the obscure or archaic English word in the first blank that is the cognate (similarly spelled), then write the more common or modern English word in the second blank. Of course, the answer key is in the back of the book!

|  | erudite or antique | common or modern |
|---|---|---|
| 1. **ver**dad | *verity* | *truth* |
| 2. culpabilidad | | |
| 3. enfermedad | | |
| 4. amistad | | |

**C.** Finally, the words that are too difficult to guess. Some of the following have common roots with English words, but can't be deciphered with confidence by the novice. To help in memorizing them, please use them in the following sentences:

*bondad*--kindness, *voluntad*--will(power), *soledad*--solitude,
*mocedad*--youth, *mitad*--half, *edad*--age, *ciudad*--city

1. Hacer errores y experimentar es cosa de ___*mocedad*___ .
2. La _____ tiene muchas personas, automóviles, y edificios; el campo tiene pocas personas, y muchos animales, ríos, montañas, y ranchos.
3. No quiero fumar otro cigarrillo, pero no tengo la fuerza de la _____.
4. A la _____de mi abuela, es difícil para ella preparar la comida para 15 personas.
5. Cuando pienso en la _____, pienso en esas personas que sirven y sacrifican.
6. También quiero ser justo; pago la _____ .
7. En Latinoamérica, se considera la _____ un estado necesario e importante, y a veces triste.

## 2. ¿Me quedo o me voy?

<u>Idiomatic expressions to learn before hearing the song</u>:
*No puedo más*--I can't take it anymore
*de la última moda*--in the latest style or fashion

*After having studied the song thoroughly, identify the indirect objects with a circle, and the reflexive pronouns by underlining them.*

Le doy _____, cariño, y pasión
Me causa envidia, pena, y depresión
  No sé si con _____ puedo más
  --Ni le gusta Cantinflas--
¿Me quedo o _____ voy?

_____ hermosa e intelectual
Soy cariñoso y _____ genial
  Te conozco  desde la niñez
  y _____ la vejez
Contigo quiero _____
¡Es más que amistad
este amor _____ mocedad!

—

Le compro _____ de la última moda
Le propongo _____ elegante y festiva boda
  Me dice --¿por qué hay tanta prisa?
  Me tormenta _____ sonrisa
Confundido yo estoy
_____ corazón le doy
Leal siempre soy
¿Me quedo o _____ voy?

Copyright Tom Blodget 1985 and 2003

## El Banco de Palabras:
These are the words that are missing in the song:

amor  de  ella  eres  estar  hasta  me  mi  muy  ropa  su  una

## Vocabulario
Below are the words and phrases of the song in English, in the order of their appearance in the song.  Fill in quickly as much of the Spanish as you know, without looking up any words in the dictionary or glossary.  Any words or phrases that you *don't* know, which

are "sandwiched" between words you *do* know, may be confidently identified by deduction.  This method eliminates the need for a dictionary.

| | |
|---|---|
| _____ | I give her |
| _____ | love |
| _____ | affection |
| _____ | and passion |
| _____ | She causes me |
| _____ | jealousy |
| _____ | troubles |
| _____ | and depression |
| _____ | I don't know |
| _____ | if |
| _____ | with her |
| _____ | I can (stand it any-) more |
| _____ | Nor, not even |
| _____ | does she like |
| _____ | Cantinflas (Mexican actor) |
| _____ | Shall I stay |
| _____ | or shall I go? |
| _____ | You are |
| _____ | beautiful |
| _____ | and intellectual |
| _____ | I am |
| _____ | affectionate |
| _____ | and witty |
| _____ | I know you |
| _____ | since |
| _____ | childhood |
| _____ | and until |
| _____ | old-age |
| _____ | with you |
| _____ | I want |
| _____ | to be |
| _____ | It's more |
| _____ | than |
| _____ | friendship |
| _____ | this love |
| _____ | young (of youth) |
| _____ | I buy her |
| _____ | clothing |
| _____ | of the latest |
| _____ | fashion |
| _____ | I propose to her |
| _____ | an elegant |
| _____ | and festive wedding |

_____She says to me
_____why
_____is there
_____so much (such)
_____(a) hurry?
_____Torments me
_____her smile
_____Confused
_____I am
_____My heart
_____I give to her
_____Loyal
_____always
_____I am
_____Shall I stay
_____or shall I go?

## Preguntas Orales.

These questions are to check for comprehension, and should be asked orally after listening to the song several times with the above activities.

1. ¿A la mujer le quiere el hombre?

2. ¿Al hombre le quiere la mujer?

3. ¿Qué *otra* persona no le gusta a la mujer?

4. ¿Hace mucho o poco tiempo que se conocen, él y ella?  ¿Cómo se sabe eso?

5. ¿Quiere el hombre casarse con ella?

6. ¿Quiere ella casarse con él ahora?

7. ¿Quiere ella casarse con él más tarde?

8. ¿Normalmente, una sonrisa es una cosa positiva.  ¿Le gusta al hombre la sonrisa de ella?  ¿Por qué no?

9. ¿Debe quedarse o irse el hombre?  ¿Si ya ella no quiere casarse con él, crees tú que ella va a querer casarse con él más tarde?  ¿Sí o no?

## I. Ser v. Estar

*Ser* and *estar* in Spanish both mean "to be," which is one of the seven (7) great wonders, or difficulties, to overcome in first year Spanish.  There is, however, a simple way to learn when to use either.  Depending on which textbook you use, *ser* has maybe 10 or more possible uses, whereas, if you exclude the present progressive tense (*estoy escuchando*=I am listening), there are *only two* cases where you will use *estar*.

The key is to use *estar* in these cases, and use ser *for every other case*!

You therefore don't have to memorize the different circumstances for the use of *ser*; just ask yourself the two basic question that satisfy *estar*: is it 1) a location, or 2) a condition ("temporary state," emotional, physical or mental state, or question of health)?

Don't necessarily assume that *ser* is "permanent" and *estar* is "temporary" as is often taught as a shorthand way of remembering, because there are genuine as well as seeming exceptions to that criteria. *Madrid está en España*, and it probably always will be for "permanent" purposes, but it's a *location*, which over-rules the "permanence" of the location. Also, some conditions are relatively permanent, like being dead (*estar muerto*) and even marriage (*estar casado*), yet *estar* is used because it is a condition or state, as in "the *state* of holy matrimony"(although *es casado* is also correct and commonly used). One may be rich and then suddenly lose all one's money in these uncertain times, but being rich is a description (*es rico*), and *ser* with descriptions over-rules *estar* even though the state of being rich is not necessarily permanent. The same is true for being young or old:

*Mi abuela es muy vieja (ser).*
*Sr. Pardo, ¡su hija es tan joven (ser)!*

However, when one notes a change, for example after not having seen someone for awhile, *estar* is used:

*¡Que alto <u>estás</u>, primo!*  How tall you are, cousin (you've recently 'shot up')!
*¡<u>Estás</u> muy bonita hoy!*  You are very pretty today (you're not always so gussied up)!

Also, in some cases the use of *ser* or *estar* with the same adjective changes the meaning of the sentence entirely:

*La comida es buena.*  The food is good (as always; you can count on it).
*La comida está buena.*  The food (that I am now eating) is good (it might have been otherwise).
*Ella no está lista.*  She's not ready.
*Ella no es muy lista.*  She's not very smart. (insightful students can see a connection between being *ready* and ultimately being considered *smart*; how can you be smart if you're never ready?)
*En este momento, sí, estoy loco. Pero no soy un loco.*  (I'm acting crazy, but I'm not crazy all the time).

**In sum, *descriptions* trump the *transitory* when using *ser*, and *conditions* and *locations* trump apparent or relative *permanence* when using *estar*.**

**A.** Of the two uses of *estar* in the song, write "location" or "condition" next to the lines:

1._____*contigo quiero estar*
2._____*confundido yo estoy*

What are the other categories for the use of the verb "to be" that would cause you to employ the verb *ser*? Although you don't absolutely have to memorize them (as a complete beginner) if you memorize the reasons for *estar*, here they are, for the record:

When to use *ser*:

1. To tell what something is made of.
*Soy hecho de carne y hueso.* I am made of flesh and bone.
2. To tell where someone or something is from.
*Soy de California.* I'm from California.
3. To describe nationality.
*Soy Estadounidense.* I'm American.
4. To describe occupation.
*Soy profesor.* I'm a professor.
5. To indicate character, quality, traits, or description.
*Soy amable, alto, inteligente, y delgado.* I'm friendly, tall, intelligent, and thin
6. Whenever using the verb "to be" other than for *condition* or *location*, especially in what some textbooks call "impersonal statements."
*Es importante llegar a tiempo. Es verdad. La fiesta es a las ocho. Es una ganga.*
It's important to arrive on time. It's true. The party is at eight. It's a bargain.
7. To tell time.
*Es la una. Son las dos.* It's one o'clock. It's two o'clock.
8. To tell the months and the seasons (*estar* can also be used *Estamos en primavera*, as if it were a location).
*Es enero. Es primavera.* It's January. It's spring.

Examples of *condition* for *estar* are:

For physical health or states:
*Estoy enfermo. Estoy bien.* I am ill. I am well.
For emotional health or states:
*¿Estás nerviosa? Usted está enojado (angry).* Are you nervous? Are you angry?
For mental health or states:
*Ese hombre está loco. Tu tío está confundido. ¿Están ustedes preparados?*
That man is nuts.    Your uncle is confused.    Are you ready?

Examples of conditions for things are:
*El coche está sucio.* The car is dirty.
*La mesa está limpia.* The table is clean.

Examples of locations for *estar* are:

*Estamos en casa.* We are at home.
*Estoy en la oficina.* I am in the office.
*El presidente está en la Casa Blanca.* The President is in the White House.

**B.** Choose either *ser* or *estar*, and conjugate it in the sentence:

1. Mi tía ___*es*___ muy alta.
2. Mi amigo Juan construye casas que _____ de madera y paja (straw).
3. La señora Vargas _____ de Venezuela.
4. El señor Alarcón _____ en Caracas, ahora, y hasta el 17 de marzo.
5. Esa casa _____ vieja.
6. ¿_____ usted mexicano o puertorriqueño?
7. La niña _____ muy feliz, porque toda la ciudad _____ de chocolate.
8. Claro que hace frío, ¡_____ invierno!
9. Vamos a llegar a clase muy tarde; ¡ya _____ las dos y cuarto!
10. Mi padre me dice que _____ importante estudiar.

## II. The -oy verbs in the yo form.

*Estar, ser, ir,* and *dar* are all irregular, but they share in common the *-y* ending in the "yo" form, where one would expect only an *-o* ending (see your own text for full conjugations):

**Estoy** *en casa.* I am at home.
**Voy** *al cine.* I'm going (I go) to the movie theater.
*Te* **doy** *mi amor.* I give you my love.
**Soy** *un hombre sincero.* I am an honest man.

**A.** Choose either *estoy, voy, doy,* or *soy* to make the sentences complete.

1. Yo no ___*voy*___ a clase porque _____ enferma.
2. Yo no _____ médico; soy enfermero.
3. --_____ aquí esperándote 40 minutos. ¿Dónde estás tú?
4. Siempre le _____ la tarea a la profesora.
5. En julio _____ a viajar a España.
6. _____ alto.
7. _____ en clase.
8. Le _____ dinero al mendigo (beggar).
9. _____ de Guadalajara.
10. _____ en Cabo San Lucas.

## III. Indirect object pronouns

Indirect object pronouns indicate *to whom* or *for whom* (or *what*) something is being done. Direct object pronouns, studied elsewhere, indicate *who* or *what* receives the action of the verb, directly. (To study the use of both pronouns together, and the object pronouns in full depth, see first the section following "Te Quiero Como Eres"). The archetypal sentence in English using both objects would be as follows. The key to understanding direct and indirect object pronouns is first simply to understand the following sentence:

*I give the ball to Pepe.*
I give what? *I give the ball.* The ball is the direct object, "what"?
To whom (or for whom…) do I give the ball?
*To Pepe.* Pepe is therefore the indirect object.

Here is the sentence in Spanish:
<u>*Le doy la pelota <u>a Pepe</u>.*</u>\*

"Le" is the indirect object pronoun, and "a Pepe" is the indirect object itself.

NOTE that, unlike English, in Spanish you MUST include the indirect object pronoun ("le") even though you use also the indirect object itself ("a Pepe"). You <u>cannot</u> say (as we do in English),
*Doy   la pelota a Pepe.*  (wrong)
I give the ball   to Pepe.

But you <u>can</u> say:
*Le        doy      la pelota.*
Him      I give   the ball (to).

without mentioning *Pepe*; perhaps it is understood that we are talking about Pepe. If it's not, we would have to include him, too, in the sentence. \*(above)

The <u>indirect object pronouns</u> in Spanish and English are:

| | |
|---|---|
| **me** -- me | **nos** -- us |
| **te** -- you (familiar singular) | **os**\* -- you (familiar plural, Spain only) |
| **le** -- him | **les** -- them (masculine) |
| **le** -- her | **les** -- them (feminine) |
| **le** -- you (formal singular) | **les** -- you (formal plural) |
| **le** -- it | **les** -- them |

\*Note that in all countries except Spain, the plural formal serves as the plural for familiars; this is true for all pronouns (subject pronoun *tú* becomes *ustedes*; indirect object pronoun te becomes *les*; direct object pronoun *te* becomes *los* or *las*). In Spain, the familiar plurals are *vosotros, os*, and *os*, respectively.

Another way of helping remember what object pronouns (whether direct or indirect) are, is to note that THEY DO NOT CONJUGATE THE VERB. This often causes trouble for beginners, especially with verbs like *gustar*. Objects, as you learned earlier in school, *receive* the action of the verb! Whereas subjects **initiate** it. (see fuller explanation of *gustar* in "Nos Gusta").

Since the indirect object is very often used with a direct object in the same sentence, we will illustrate such a sentence here. (For a fuller treatment of both direct and indirect object pronouns, see the explanation in "Te Quiero Como Eres").

"I serve coffee to my customers."

"I" is the <u>subject</u> which conjugates and drives the <u>verb</u> "serve", and the <u>direct object</u> is the "coffee" ("what"), which is given to the "customers"--the <u>indirect object</u>.

So in English the sentence is written S--V--  DO--  Ind.O.
                                                    I--serve--coffee--to my customers.

In Spanish the sentence is written (S*)—Ind.O. Pronoun      --V--  DO--  Ind.O.
                                                    (Yo*optional)--les         --sirvo--café--a mis clientes.

If you study the above sentence, you will know how to do many other sentences in Spanish correctly...

**A.** Below you will be given the indirect object (the person or thing--but usually a person) in the sentence provided. You will need to put the indirect object *pronoun* in front of the verb, in the space provided. The prepositional pronouns <u>underlined</u> should make this a very easy exercise (see page 39 for chart of prepositional pronouns). The idea is to get used to the *placement* of the pronouns, which is unlike the English usage.

**A.** Clues for using the correct pronoun are the <u>prepositional pronouns underlined</u> in the sentences (see "Nos Gusta" for treatment of prepositional pronouns)

1. _____ manda una carta <u>a nosotras</u> nuestro gran amigo Carlos.
2. _____ voy a dar un regalo <u>a usted</u>.
3. _____ soy fiel <u>a ti</u>.
4. _____ doy cien dólares <u>a ustedes</u> por 10 horas de trabajo.
5. _____ cuento <u>a ustedes</u> de mis hazañas en la guerra.
6. Siempre cuando la visito, mi hija _____ encuentra un hotel <u>para mí</u> en el centro.
7. _____ compro <u>a ella</u> ropa de la última moda.
8. ¿_____ gusta <u>a ti</u> Cantinflas?
9. _____ doy <u>a ella</u> mi corazón y mi dinero, pero no es suficiente.
10. _____ mando <u>a vosotros</u> mi amor.

## IV. Estar + past participle (regular) *(Estoy confundido=I am confused)*

This concept is <u>easy</u> because it is identical in English. You conjugate the verb "to be" and connect it to the past participle, whose rules for formation in Spanish are simple:
1) verbs ending in *-ar* have that ending replaced with *-ado*

2) verbs ending in *-er* or *-ir* have that ending replaced with *-ido* (<u>never</u> *-edo*; both are replaced with *-ido*).

There are about 15 important irregular exceptions to this for beginning and intermediate learners, which won't concern us here. The following participles are all <u>regular</u>. Note also that even though the conjugated form of the verb is reflexive, the reflexive pronouns are not used in this construction.

1. enojar(se)--to be angry, annoyed
2. confundir(se)--to be confused
3. ocupar(se)--to be occupied, busy
4. cansar(se)--to be tired
5. enamorar(se)--to be in love
6. enloquecer(se)--to go crazy
7. casar(se)--to be married
8. aburrir(se)--to be bored
9. entusiasmar(se)--to be excited
10. decepcionar(se)--to be disappointed
11. distraer(se)--to be distracted
12. liberar(se)--to free oneself

Note that if you are female, the participle ends in "-a": *Estoy preocupad<u>a</u>*. I'm worried.

**A.** Using the rule for how the past participle is formed (above), please write the ten infinitives above in their past participle form, starting with "Estoy…".

Masculino:
1. _____*Estoy enojado*_____
2. _____
3. _____
4. _____
5. _____
6. _____
Femenino:
7. _____*Estoy casada*_____
8. _____
9. _____
10. _____
11. _____
12. _____

# V. Nouns ending in *-sión*

All nouns ending in *-ssion* or *-sion* in English are equivalent to *-sión* in Spanish, and they are always feminine. Note that there are, however, some words in Spanish ending in *-sión* that have other endings in English (e.g., *presión* = *press<u>ure</u>*)

la impre<u>sión</u> = the impre<u>ssion</u>
la vi<u>sión</u> = (the) vi<u>sion</u>

**A.** Here are some recognizable words.  Insert them in the blanks.

*confusión  hipertensión  división  obsesión  invasión*
*precisión  compasión  decisión  impresión  opresión*

1. Mi abuela es muy vieja y sufre la __*hipertensión*__ .
2. En la escuela aprendemos la multiplicación y la _____ .
3. Algunos pobres en el mundo resisten la _____ .
4. Tenemos que tomar una _____ si queremos comprar la casa o no.
5. La _____ del país enemigo ocurre mañana por la mañana.
6. Si uno tiene _____, siente profundamente.
7. El contrario de la la *claridad* es la _____ .
8. Esa persona me da una buena _____. Me gusta.
9. La persona que repite el mismo error continuamente puede padecer (sufrir) de una _____ clínica.
10. Dicen que las bombas y mísiles llegan a su blanco (target) con mucha _____, pero yo no sé.

**B.** In Spanish, *-ción is invariably -tion in English.*

*satisfacción  excepción  investigación  constitución  destrucción  construcción*
*polución  distribución  atención  emoción  pronunciación*

1. "La mano" es un ejemplo de la __*excepción*__ a la regla del uso "masculino/feminino."
2. La economía es la _____ de los bienes en la sociedad
3. La _____ es un documento legal importantísimo, que garantiza los derechos de los ciudadanos del país.
4. En la clase, tienes que prestar _____, o no aprendes nada.
5. Durante las guerras, hay mucha _____. Después de las guerras, hay mucha (6) _____ .
7. Muchas personas basan sus decisiones y opiniones en la _____ y no en la razón.
8. Si haces buen trabajo, sientes una gran _____ .
9. La _____ entra en el aire, el agua, y la tierra, y finalmente en la comida que consumimos.
10. En español, la _____ es fácil, porque la lengua se escribe tal como se dice.
11. Tienen que hacer una _____ sobre los crímenes.

# VI. Suffixes: *-ez*

**A.** The suffix *-ez* often (but not always) equals *-ity*, as in the first four words in the list. The same can't be said for the last two words, since they have no common root with modern English, so their translations are given. Choose one word for each sentence below.

*estupidez aridez madurez rigidez   vejez* (old age)   *niñez* (childhood)

1.  Antonio no tiene la ____*madurez*___; todavía se comporta como un niño mimado (spoiled).
2.  La _____ de su opinión no permite alternativas.
3.  Conozco a Ana desde la _____.
4.  En la _____, quiero poder decir que "la vida es buena."
5.  No podemos plantar aquí por la _____ de la tierra.
6.  Por la _____de los responsables, todos tenemos que sufrir.

# VII. Reflexive verbs (me quedo, me voy, etc.)

Spanish has a lot of verbs that are "reflexive", and therefore require the reflexive pronouns *me/te/se* (singular), and *nos/os/se* (plural). For an English speaker, this is generally a pain in the brain, at first.

Grammatically, the way to use them is just like with the subject pronouns you may have already memorized by now: *yo, tú, él, ella, usted, nosotros, vosotros, ellos, ellas*, and *ustedes*. The reflexive pronouns march in "lock-step" with these, so to speak  Let's chart them out. Please note how the pronouns correspond, in terms of which of the six little boxes they are in.

**Reflexive pronouns**

| | |
|---|---|
| *me* | *nos* |
| *te* | *os* |
| *se* | *se* |

**Subject pronouns**

| | |
|---|---|
| yo | nosotros/as |
| tú | vosotros/as |
| él | ellos |
| ella | ellas |
| usted | ustedes |

As you may know, the subject pronouns may be omitted from speech or writing if it is understood which person is referred to:

*Yo lavo el coche.* → *Lavo el coche.*  I wash the car.

(The reason is because the *"-o"* in *lavo* already indicates that it is "I" who does the washing.)

The reflexive pronoun, however, may <u>never</u> be <u>omitted</u>.  It goes directly before the conjugated verb:

*(Yo) me lavo las manos.*  I wash (by myself) my hands.
*(Tú) te lavas las manos.*  You wash (by yourself) your hands.
*(Usted) se lava las manos.*  You wash (by yourself) your hands.
*(Él) se lava las manos.*  He washes (by himself) his hands.
*(Ella) se lava las manos.*  She washes (by herself) her hands.
*(Nosotros) nos lavamos las manos.*  We wash (by ourselves) our hands.
*(Vosotros) os laváis las manos.*  You all wash (by yourselves) your hands.
*(Ustedes) se lavan las manos.*  You wash (by yourselves) your hands.
*(Ellos) se lavan las manos.*  They wash (by themselves) their hands.
*(Ellas) se lavan las manos.*  They wash (by themselves) their hands.

By meditating on the above examples, you will know how to conjugate any reflexive verb.

There seem to be various grades or types of reflexive verbs.  Some make sense in their own way, and others don't seem to.

**1.** The easiest type of reflexive verbs to understand are those which indicate actions done to "oneself"--*myself, yourself, himself, herself, itself, ourselves, yourselves, and themselves.*  For example, "<u>I dry myself</u> (off) with a towel." *Me seco con una toalla.*  "<u>You dry yourself</u>..." *Te secas...etcetera.*  This can be learned systematically and is not a great problem for the intermediate or even the attentive beginning student.

**2.** Some reflexive verbs may also be used non-reflexively, with a direct object.  For example, one can hide "oneself", and of course one can also hide "something else":

*Me escondo detrás de la cortina.*  <u>I('ll) hide</u> (<u>myself</u>) behind the curtain.
*Escondo el remoto detrás de la cortina.*  <u>I('ll) hide</u> <u>the remote</u> behind the curtain.

It is natural for an English speaker to want to omit the *Me* in the first sentence, because "I'll hide myself" seems redundant in English.  Why can't you just say "I'll hide"?  Well, the answer is because, in Spanish, *they don't do it that way.*  You have to include the reflexive.  And the best way to learn which verbs are reflexive is to consult your *501* or *201 verbs* reference book, or your standard text.

**3.** What *is* problematic for all learners are the many verbs in Spanish that are reflexive for no compelling reason: *decidir* o *decidirse* are both listed in the dictionary, with no compelling difference in meaning.  *Imaginar(se)* is another example of this.

**4**. Oftentimes however, adding the reflexive pronoun *changes the meaning of the verb.* Note the difference in meaning in the examples below:

Reflexive: *Nos quedamos hasta las nueve*: We'll stay (or we stayed) until 9.
Not reflexive: *Quedamos a las nueve*: We'll meet at 9.

Reflexive: *Me voy*. I'm going (no destination given; the person is just vacating that spot).
Not reflexive: *Voy al cine*. I'm going to the movie theater (without reflexive pronoun, a destination is *required*).

There's a whole set of reflexive verbs that must be taught to the beginning Spanish student because they involve personal hygiene and the daily (especially morning) routine: waking up, getting out of bed, taking a shower, drying off, brushing one's teeth, washing one's hands or face, shaving, combing one's hair, getting dressed, and preparing food-- basic activities that all happen to require the use of the reflexive.

The difficulty for the student is that the English literal translation of these activities sounds like the following: "I myself wake up," "I myself get up," "I wash myself my hands," "I brush myself my teeth," etc., which makes the student want to give sarcastic congratulations for the Spanish speaker who has accomplished these difficult tasks "all by him- or herself." It sounds redundant in English, but in Spanish the reflexive pronoun **cannot** be omitted, and will sound **incorrect** if it is.

Here are the verbs conjugated in the first person "yo" form. Please insert in each sentence so that it makes sense. Not all will be used, and those used will only be used once.

Por la mañana, antes de salir de la casa:

*me despierto*--I wake up
*me levanto (de la cama)*--I get up (out of bed)
*me ducho*--I take a shower
*me seco (con una toalla)*--I dry off (with a towel)
*me cepillo los dientes*--I brush my teeth
*me afeito*--I shave
*me peino (el cabello)*--I comb (my hair)
*me pongo la ropa*--I put my clothes on (also: *me visto* without saying la ropa)
*me preparo el desayuno*--I prepare breakfast (for myself)

Por la tarde, después de volver a casa:

*me quito los zapatos*--I take off my shoes
*me lavo las manos y la cara*--I wash my hands and face
*me quito la ropa*--I take off my clothes
*me pongo los pijamas*--I put on my pajamas

*me acuesto*--I go to bed (literally *I lay myself down on my back*)
*me duermo*--I fall asleep (*duermo* by itself means "I sleep"; adding the reflexive pronoun makes it a sudden experience)

Students may do a storyboard illustration using "stick-men", "found" images, or artistic drawings to illustrate the above routines. Other possibilities are doing a video, miming, or "charades" in front of the class.

**A.** Using the verbs conjugated above, fill in the blanks, always using the "yo" form.

1. Para mantener un hálito agradable, __*me cepillo*__ los dientes.
2. Cuando tengo sueño, a las once de la noche, _____.
3. Porque tengo cabello muy largo, _____ no sólo por la mañana sino muchas veces durante el día.
4. En la cocina, a las siete y media, _____ el desayuno.
5. No duermo con la ropa que llevo durante el día ¡claro! Antes de acostarme, me quito la ropa y _____ los pijamas.
6. Porque yo trabajo en restaurante, siempre _____ las manos después de usar el baño. En el baño hay un letrero que dice: *Según la ley del Estado de California y por consideración a todos, hay que lavarse las manos después de usar el baño.*
7. Yo _____ con agua muy caliente por la mañana por quince minutos; después de tantos años en el campo, me encanta una regadera con agua bien caliente.
8. Es costumbre en algunas casas no llevar zapatos dentro de la casa, porque los zapatos están sucios por haber pisado fuera en lugares sucios; así que cuando entro en mi casa, después de cerrar la puerta, siempre _____ los zapatos.
9. Generalmente, en Europa, las mujeres no se afeitan los sobacos (underarms). Porque soy norteamericana, sí _____ los sobacos, porque todo el mundo aquí lo hace, y si una mujer no lo hace, sus amigas van a pensar que ella es rara (strange).
10. ¿Por cuánto tiempo se queda usted en la cama, entre el momento en que se despierta y en que se levanta? Yo casi siempre _____ inmediatamente después de despertarme.

# 3. La Fiesta (tiene que ser divertida)

Idiomatic expressions to learn before hearing the song:
*¡claro qué sí!* -- of course
*¡vete!* -- Scram! Get outta here!
*lo que tú quieras* -- whatever you want
*un montón* -- a whole lot, a ton
*m'ija -- slang, contraction of 'mi hija'* -- my daughter
*a bajo interés* -- at a low interest rate

Este sábado tenemos_____, Pepa
Para mi cumpleaños
Yo les quiero preparar una cena _____
a los invitados
Así que hay que hacer las compras, piba
Vamos ya al _____
Compramos lo que necesitamos, nena
Hasta el pastel encomendado
¡claro que sí!

De la _____ precisamos toda, hembra
¡Este es un banquete!
Queremos lomo y merluza y_____, chica
Y chorizo, ¡ya vete!
Oh, _____ queremos bebida, chavala
Champán, cerveza, _____, y sidra
Agua, gaseosa, y zumo, _____,
Y refrescos para todo el mundo,
¡Lo que tú quieras!

*La fiesta _____ que ser divertida*
*La fiesta _____ que ser bien acudida*
*Con la _____ bailando y cantando, Pepita*
*Y tomando y comiendo un montón, señorita*

Lo que queremos para la ensalada, moza
Son _____ y lechuga
También jamón, vinagre y aceite, tronca
_____ algunas aceitunas
También pimienta, sal, y cebolla, doncella
Para darle una _____ sazón*          (**masc. en México*)
La mezclamos en esta olla, _____
Y por encima exprimimos limón
De ese árbol    allí

*La fiesta _____ que ser divertida*

*La fiesta _____ que ser bien acudida*
*Con la _____ bailando y cantando, Pepita*
*Y tomando y comiendo un montón, señorita*

—

*La fiesta _____ que ser divertida*
*La fiesta _____ que ser bien acudida*
*Con la _____ bailando y cantando, Pepita*
*Y tomando y comiendo un montón, señorita*

Para picar necesitamos las tapas, m'ija
Como _____ ali oli
Mejillones y tortillas españolas, *baby*
¿No tenemos _____ boli?
Creo ya que eso es_____, damisela
Vamos a ver si tengo las pelas*                    (*slang in Spain for *pesetas*)
Si no las _____ tienes tarjeta, tía
Que nos compra todo lo que anhelas*               (*more often would be *anheles*)
¡A bajo interés!

Coyright Tom Blodget 2003

## El Banco de Palabras:
These are the words that are missing in the song:

carne  con  fiesta  fuerte  gente  grande  muchacha  niña  otro  patatas  pollo
supermercado  también  tengo  tiene  todo  tomates  vino

## Vocabulario

Below are the words and phrases of the song in English, in the order of their appearance in the song. Fill in quickly as much of the Spanish as you know, without looking up any words in the dictionary or glossary. Any words or phrases that you *don't* know, which are "sandwiched" between words you *do* know, may be confidently identified by deduction. This method eliminates the need for a dictionary.

_____this Saturday
_____we have
_____party, Pepa
_____for my birthday
_____I want to prepare (for them)
_____a dinner
_____big
_____for the guests

_____ So

_____ we have to (one has to)

_____ do the shopping, kid (pibe masc, Arg.)

_____ We'll* go (*present tense = immediate future, too)

_____ now

_____ to the supermarket

_____ We'll* buy

_____ what we need, girl

_____ even

_____ the cake

_____ specially requested

_____ of course!

_____ As for meat ("of the meat")

_____ we need

_____ everything, girl ("female")

_____ this is a banquet

_____ we want

_____ porkloin

_____ and hake (a white fish common in Spain)

_____ and chicken, girl

_____ and sausage

_____ now scram!

_____ oh, also

_____ we want

_____ drinks, lassie

_____ champage, beer

_____ wine and cider

_____ water, soda

_____ and juice*, child    (*jugo en LatinoAmérica)

_____ and beverages

_____ for everyone

_____ whatever you want!

_____ the party

_____ has to be

_____ fun

_____ the party

_____ has to be

_____ well-attended

_____ with people

_____ dancing and singing, Pepita

_____ and drinking

_____ and eating a lot, missy

_____ what we want

_____ for the salad, young lady

_____ are tomatoes and lettuce

_____ also ham

| | |
|---|---|
| _____ | vinegar and oil, |
| _____ | dude (literally "trunk," Spain, ca. 1980s) |
| _____ | with some olives |
| _____ | also pepper, salt |
| _____ | and onion, maiden/damsel |
| _____ | in order to |
| _____ | give it |
| _____ | a strong |
| _____ | flavor/taste |
| _____ | We'll* mix it |
| _____ | in this pot, girl |
| _____ | and on top |
| _____ | we'll* squeeze |
| _____ | lemon |
| _____ | from that tree, there |

… (repeat chorus; instrumental; repeat chorus)

| | |
|---|---|
| _____ | for |
| _____ | snacking |
| _____ | we need "tapas", my daughter |
| _____ | like garlicky potatoes |
| _____ | mussels |
| _____ | and "Spanish tortillas" baby (potato-onion- |

scrambled egg "omelet" not to be confused with Mexican style tortilla bread)

| | |
|---|---|
| _____ | don't we have |
| _____ | another pen? |
| _____ | I think now |
| _____ | that |
| _____ | that |
| _____ | is all, damsel |
| _____ | Let's see |
| _____ | if I have the cash |
| _____ | if |
| _____ | I don't have it ("them") |
| _____ | you have a (credit) card, "aunt" (slang in Spain) |
| _____ | that'll buy* us |
| _____ | all |
| _____ | that you (do in fact) desire |

## Preguntas Orales.

These questions are to check for comprehension, and should be asked orally after listening to the song several times with the above activities.

1. ¿En qué día de la semana es la fiesta?

2. ¿Qué ocasión van a celebrar en ese día? ¿Un *aniversario de boda* o un *cumpleaños*?

3. ¿Van a tener *mucha* comida o *poca* comida?

4. ¿Van a tener *mucha* bebida o *poca* bebida?

5. ¿Adónde van para comprar la comida y la bebida?

6. ¿Son vegetarianos (sí o no)? ¿Les gusta la carne (sí o no)?

7. ¿Van a comprar solamente bebidas alcohólicas, o van a comprar todo tipo de bebidas?

8. ¿Quieren que vengan (use hand gesture) *muchas* personas o *pocas* personas a la fiesta?

9. ¿Qué van a hacer los invitados en la fiesta? *¿Dormir* o *bailar*? *¿Cantar* o *mirar la tele*?

10. ¿Tomate, lechuga, y cebolla son ingredientes de *la paella* o de *una ensalada*?

11. ¿Van a comprar el limón en el supermercado, o van a cogerlo del árbol cerca de la casa, probablemente en el patio?

12. ¿Qué son algunos ejemplos de "tapas" en la canción?

13. ¿Quién tiene una tarjeta de crédito, el hombre o la mujer?

14. ¿Crees que el hombre tiene dinero suficiente para pagar la comida y la bebida (sí o no)?

15. ¿Quién va a pagar (gesture by beating fist in hand) las compras, el hombre con sus "pelas" o la mujer con su tarjeta de crédito?

# I. El Vocabulario de la Comida y la Bebida

**A.** Write 'C' for 'comida' (food) or 'B' for 'bebida' (drink) next to the vocabulary found in the song (*these exercises may also be done orally in the classroom, or with a partner*):

1 _*B*_ agua con gas/agua mineral
2____ el champán
3____ el chorizo
4____ el jamón
5____ el limón
6____ el lomo
7____ el pastel
8____ el pollo
9____ el refresco
10____ el vino
11____ el zumo

12___la carne
13___la cebolla
14___la cerveza
15___la ensalada
16___la lechuga
17___la merluza
18___la sidra
19___la tortilla española
20___las aceitunas
21___las patatas *ali oli*
22___las tapas
23___los mejillones
24___los tomates

**B.** Now label the following by food category:

CA=carne
M=marisco
BA=bebida alcohólica
R=refresco (no alcohólico)
F=fruta
V=vegetal
P=postre
CO=condimento

1_*R*_agua con gas/agua mineral/agua gaseosa
2___el aceite
3___el champán
4___el chorizo
5___el jamón
6___el limón
7___el lomo
8___el pastel
9___el pollo
10___el vinagre
11___el vino
12___el zumo
13___la cebolla
14___la cerveza
15___la ensalada
16___la lechuga
17___la merluza
18___la pimienta
19___la sal
20___la sidra
21___las aceitunas

22___ las patatas *ali oli*
23___ los mejillones
24___ los tomates

## II. Chavalas y Chavales

**A.** Match the names for females with the males. (*Damisela*, as in *la damisela en apuros*-- "the damsel in distress"--doesn't have a masculine equivalent). First write the matching letter, and then write the masculine equivalent.

| | | |
|---|---|---|
| 1. _J-Pepito_ Pepita | | A. chaval |
| 2._____ piba | | B. chico |
| 3._____ nena | | C. doncel |
| 4._____ hembra | | D. m'ijo |
| 5._____ chica | | E. macho |
| 6._____ chavala | | F. mozo |
| 7._____ niña | | G. muchacho |
| 8._____ señorita | | H. nene (*la Argentina/Uruguay, España) |
| 9._____ moza | | I. niño |
| 10._____ tronca | | J. Pepito |
| 11._____ doncella | | K. pibe (*la Argentina/Uruguay) |
| 12._____ muchacha | | L. señorito |
| 13._____ m'ija | | M. tío (**España) |
| 14._____ tía | | N. tronco (**España) |

## III. Demonstrative adjectives *(este, esta, eso)*

Let's start with the <u>feminine</u> forms, as they are completely consistent. They all end in *"-a"* or *"-as"*:

| | |
|---|---|
| *esta*--this | *estas*--these |
| *esa*--that | *esas*--those |

The <u>masculine</u> forms, one would expect, would all have *"-o"* or *"-os"*. But *no*… The singular ends in *"-e"*.

| | |
|---|---|
| est**e**--this | estos--these |
| es**e**--that | esos--those |

The reason for this is that the *neuter* form of "this" and "that" ends in *"-o"*.

| |
|---|
| *esto--this (gender unknown)* |
| *eso--that (gender unknown)* |

It is logical to have a neuter form, because one is often asking the question *¿Qué es esto?* "What is this?" or *¿Qué es eso?* "What is that?" and since in Spanish every identified noun has a gender, the <u>unknown nouns</u> would have to have either 1) a "neuter," or 2) a "default" masculine that ignored sex. In Spanish, with these adjectives, the first path was taken.

They are called *demonstrative* adjectives because the speaker is "demonstrating" or "showing" the noun in question: *this* book, *these* papers, *that* car, *those* desks (*este* libro, *estos* papeles, *ese* coche, *esos* pupitres); or, in the feminine: *this* house, *these* blouses, *that* lady, *those* clouds (esta casa, estas blusas, esa mujer, esas nubes). Imagine a person standing next to a building, pointing at it, and saying, *Este edificio data del siglo catorce...(this building dates from the 14^{th} century...).* The tour guide is *pointing out* to us the building.

<u>Keys to memorizing the demonstrative adjectives:</u>
*1)* In English, *this, these, that,* and *those* all begin with *"th-";*
2) In Spanish, "this and these" (*este/esta* and *estos/estas*) all have a 't' in them, indicating closeness; subtract the 't', and it's farther away: "that and those" (*ese/esa, esos/esas*).

**A.** The following exercises ask you to use either the "close" or "far away" adjective. You also have to keep in mind to use the feminine and masculine, as well as the singular and plural. You are given nouns that by their nature are usually either closer or further away, with their definite articles (*el, la, los, las*) so you can tell the gender and number (*el coche* (m.) = *este coche*). You want to replace those articles with the demonstrative adjectives that correspond in number and gender.

| Cerca--near; "aquí" a mano--close at hand | Lejos--far; "allí"--farther away |
|---|---|
| 1. el coche  *este coche* | 1.las nubes  *esas nubes* |
| 2. la lámpara | 2.las montañas |
| 3. las ideas | 3.la persona |
| 4. la casa | 4.los edificios |
| 5. los libros | 5.el mosquito |
| 6. la computadora | 6.la escuela |
| 7. el teléfono | 7.el tren |
| 8. los árboles | 8.la confusión |
| 9. el papel | 9.los españoles |
| 10.el bolígrafo | 10.la fiesta |

## IV. Tener que/hay que

Both *tener que* and *hay que* express obligation, what one must do. With *tener*, it is personalized, and with *haber (hay)*, it is impersonal. When one uses *hay*, one is indicating that someone within earshot or associated with the group *has to do* the task. One could just as well use *tener*, but that would be more specific and direct. A good example would be how direct the speaker would want to be, regarding something like, say, paying taxes.  If someone tells you they aren't going to file, you could personalize it (*tener*) and say, "but you have to," (*tienes que pagar los impuestos…*) or you could say it impersonally (*haber*), in the sense of "we all know that one has to; it's not up for discussion" (*hay que pagar los impuestos…*)

*Hay que* is used impersonally, and therefore has no "person," so needs not be further conjugated.  It is always followed by the infinitive:

*Hay que <u>lavar</u> los platos.  One has to wash the dishes.*
*Hay que <u>sufrir</u>.  One must suffer.*
*Hay que <u>hacerlo</u>.  One has to do it.*

With *tener*, you have to conjugate the verb in any of its six forms:

"<u>We</u> have to do it,"/*<u>Tenemos</u> que hacerlo.*
"<u>She</u> has to do it/*<u>Tiene</u> que hacerlo <u>ella</u>.*

**A.** Write the Spanish below the English:

1.  I have to do it.

_____

2.  One has to do it.

_____

3.  We have to go now.

_____

4.  Do you have to work today?

_____

5.  This book must be read (*this book* must come last in the Spanish translation.)

_____

# V. Por y Para

Note the following variety of usages in the examples of these prepositions (in parentheses).
Note also how many different translations *por* and *para* have in their English equivalents, depending on the sentence.  These examples demonstrate the most common usages.

**Para:**
1. Estudio español <u>para</u> mejor entender mis colegas en el trabajo. **("in order to")**
   *I study Spanish <u>in order to</u> better understand my work colleagues.*
2. Este regalo es <u>para</u> ti. **(intended recipient)**
   *This gift is <u>for</u> you.*
3. Trabajo <u>para</u> una compañía que nos paga bien a los empleados.  **(to work for)**
   *I work <u>for</u> a company that pays its employees well.*
4. Salimos <u>para</u> las montañas mañana. **(destination)**
   *We leave <u>for</u> the mountains tomorrow.*

5. Tengo que terminar este ensayo <u>para</u> el viernes. **(deadline)**
   *I have to finish this essay <u>by</u> Friday.*
6. <u>Para</u> ser tan joven, Alfonso tiene muy buenos modales. **(to compare to expectations)**
   *For such a young person, Alfonso has very good manners.*
7. <u>Para mí</u>, mirar la televisión toda la tarde es una pérdida de tiempo. **(opinion)**
   *<u>In my opinion</u>, watching TV all afternoon is a waste of time.*

**Por:**
1. Te vendo este puente <u>por</u> cien dólares. **(exchange)**
   *I'll sell you this bridge <u>for</u> a hundred dollars.*
2. Caminamos <u>por</u> el parque todos los días. **(through)**
   *We walk <u>through</u> the park every day.*
3. --El restaurante está <u>por</u> aquí--¡allí está! **(imprecise location)**
   *"The restaurant is <u>around</u> here—there it is!*
4. Vamos a ver la película <u>por</u> la tarde. **(imprecise time)**
   *We're going to see the movie <u>in</u> the afternoon.*
5. Vamos a estar en Venezuela <u>por</u> tres semanas. **(duration of time)**
   *We're going to be in Venezuela <u>for</u> three weeks.*
6. *Don Quijote de la Mancha* fue escrito <u>por</u> Miguel de Cervantes. **(authorship)**
   Don Quijote de la Mancha *was written <u>by</u> Miguel de Cervantes.*
7. <u>Por</u> no tener dinero suficiente, Pepe no puede comprar la entrada. **(cause)**
   *<u>For</u> not having enough money (<u>because</u> he didn't have…), Pepe couldn't buy the ticket.*
8. Todo lo que hago es <u>por</u> ti. **(sake)**
   *Everything I do is <u>for</u> you(r sake).*
9. Esta motocicleta puede llegar a los 150 kilómetros <u>por</u> hora. **("per")**
   *This motorcycle can reach 150 km <u>per</u> hour.*
10. Vamos <u>por</u> tren. **(means,** or *how* **done)**
   We're going <u>by</u> train.

**A. Para.**  Write the number for the reason for the usage (each used once).

   1.  intended recipient    2. destination   3. deadline   4. "in order to"
   5.  to compare to expectations   6. opinion   7. to work for   8. purpose

   1.  _____ <u>Para</u> ser tan pobre, usted es muy generosa.
   2.  _____ Tienen que hacer esta tarea <u>para</u> el lunes.
   3.  _____ Yo solamente como comida saludable <u>para</u> conservar la salud.
   4.  _____ <u>Para</u> nosotros, no es buena idea gastar mucho dinero en cosas que
       realmente no necesitamos.
   5.  _____ Mi padre trabaja <u>para</u> una fábrica que produce palitos.
   6.  _____ Salen <u>para</u> Santiago de Compostela la semana que viene.
   7.  _____ --Este dinero es <u>para</u> usted; lo va a necesitar.
   8.  _____ Ese dinero es para pagar la luz (the electric bill)

**B. Por.** Write the number for the reason for the usage (each used once).

9. exchange  10. through  11. imprecise location  12. imprecise time  13. duration of time
14. authorship  15. cause  16. sake  17. "per"  18. means, *how* done

1. _____ Ganamos noventa dólares por día.
2. _____ *Tiempo de Silencio* fue escrito por Luis Martín-Santos.
3. _____ Le doy a usted cincuenta dólares por ese caballo.
4. _____ Me gusta estudiar por la noche.
5. _____ Vamos a pasar por muchos pueblos pequeños y aldeas antiguas.
6. _____ Los padres trabajan por los niños.
7. _____ Hay varias tiendas de ropa por esa parte de la ciudad.
8. _____ El partido entre los Gigantes y los Atléticos fue cancelado por la lluvia.
9. _____ Voy a estudiar por tres horas antes de preparar la cena.
10. _____ No vamos por avión; vamos en coche.

**C.** Give the **reason** for the use of *por* o *para*, of the **18** possible shown above.

1. _15. cause_____ No trabajamos durante la tarde por el calor.
2. _____ Vivo para comer, y como para vivir.
3. _____ *La Flor de Potosí* fue escrito por Tom Blodget.
4. _____ Te doy mi guitarra por tu bicicleta.
5. _____ Para ellos, vale la pena ir a la conferencia.
6. _____ Esperamos el autobús por 45 minutos.
7. _____ La pelota pasó por la ventana de la Sra Pérez que vive al
lado.  Ella siempre habla del peligro de vivir tan cerca del estadio de béisbol.
8. _____ No coman esa comida; es para la fiesta mañana.
9. _____ Me gusta correr por la mañana.
10. _____ Yo trabajo para el departamento de obras públicas.

# VI. The gerund or present participle *(-iendo and -ando)*

A. In the song there are four instances of the present participle used in the
song in just two successive lines.  In English, a gerund is the *-ing* form of
the verb infinitive (*to talk, talking*); in Spanish, the *regular* form of the
gerund (as in this song) is *-ando* for -AR verbs, and *-iendo* for -ER and -IR
verbs (*hablar, hablando; querer, queriendo*).

**A.** Write the present participles here:

**B.** Now write the verb infinitives they came from:

1 _bailando_____
2 _____
3 _____
4 _____

1 _bailar_____
2 _____
3 _____
4 _____

## 4. Nos Gusta

*Entre las personas tenemos _____ en común*
*De los gustos varios hay, pero _____ del corazón*
*somos seres*
*con la luz*
*que _____ luce*
*Queremos las mismas cosas--el bienestar,*
*_____, comunidad, y un buen hogar*

Me gusta la vida
Me gusta el _____
de vivir y amar
Me gusta _____ y pensar
Me gusta hablar y cantar

Te gustan las chicas
Te gustan los _____
y te gusta salir
pero a ti no te gusta bailar
ni _____ te gusta lucir

   A todos   nos gusta _____ varias cosas
   porque somos   talentosos y únicos _____

A mi amiga le gusta
al _____ y al béisbol
y al tenis jugar*
a ella le gusta _____
a ella le gusta viajar

A mis primos les gusta
montar a _____
y animales criar*
Les gusta _____ en el campo
Les gusta el aire tomar*

   A todos   nos gusta _____ varias cosas
   porque somos   talentosos y únicos _____

—

A nosotros nos gusta
a la _____ entera
a las dos almorzar*

Nos gusta en _____ estar*
Nos gusta también conversar

*Entre las personas tenemos* _____ *en común*
*De los gustos varios hay, pero* _____ *del corazón*
*somos seres*
*con la luz*
*que* _____ *luce*
*Queremos las mismas cosas--el bienestar,*
_____*, comunidad, y un buen hogar*    *(*all cases of* hyperbaton)

copyright Tom Blodget 1990, and May 11, 2001

## El Banco de Palabras:
These are the words that are missing in the song:

algo  arte  bailes  caballo  casa  comida  dentro  familia
golf  hacer  leer  pintar  siempre  tampoco  todos  vivir

## Vocabulario

Below are the words and phrases of the song in English, in the order of their appearance
in the song.  Fill in quickly as much of the Spanish as you know, without looking up any
words in the dictionary or glossary.  Any words or phrases that you *don't* know, which
are "sandwiched" between words you *do* know, may be confidently identified by
deduction.  This method eliminates the need for a dictionary.

_____among
_____(all) the people
_____we have something
_____in common
_____of tastes
_____various/many
_____there are
_____but inside
_____of the heart
_____we are beings
_____with the light
_____that always shines
_____we want the same things
_____well being
_____food, community
_____and a good home
_____I like life
_____the art
_____of living and loving

| | I like |
|---|---|
| _____ | to read and to think |
| _____ | to speak and to sing |
| _____ | you like girls |
| _____ | you like dances |
| _____ | and you like to "go out" |
| _____ | but |
| _____ | you don't like to dance |
| _____ | nor either |
| _____ | we all ("to all") |
| _____ | we like to do |
| _____ | a variety of |
| _____ | things |
| _____ | because we are |
| _____ | talented and unique |
| _____ | everyone |
| _____ | my friend likes |
| _____ | golf and baseball |
| _____ | and tennis |
| _____ | to play |
| _____ | she likes to paint |
| _____ | she likes to travel |
| _____ | my cousins like |
| _____ | to ride horses |
| _____ | and to raise animals |
| _____ | they like to live |
| _____ | in the country(side) |
| _____ | they like to take the air |

…(repeat bridge)

| _____ | we like |
|---|---|
| _____ | --the family whole-- |
| _____ | at two o'clock |
| _____ | to eat lunch |
| _____ | we like |
| _____ | at home ("in" home) |
| _____ | to be |
| _____ | we like |
| _____ | also |
| _____ | to chat |

(…repeat intro verse)

## Preguntas Orales

These questions are to check for comprehension, and should be asked orally after listening to the song several times with the above activities.

1.  Según el autor, ¿cuáles son algunas de las cosas que todo el mundo quiere, o requiere?

2.  Aunque le gustan los bailes a su amigo, ¿por qué dice también que NO le gusta bailar? Si no le gusta bailar, ¿por qué le gustan los bailes?  ¿Puede ser que no sabe bailar (sí o no)?  ¿Puede ser que es tímido (sí o no)?  ¿Puede ser que le gustan las chicas, y va a los bailes porque las chicas están allí (sí o no)?

3.  ¿Es verdad que todos nosotros tenemos un talento?

4.  A su amiga le gustan los deportes--el golf, el béisbol, el tenis.  ¿Es ella *atlética* o *perezosa*?

5.  ¿Les gusta más *la ciudad* o *el campo* a los primos?

6.  ¿Les gustan más a los primos *los videojuegos* o *las vacas*, probablemente?

7.  *¿A qué hora* almuerza esa familia?

8.  ¿Les gusta pasar mucho tiempo comiendo y conversando (sí o no)?

9.  En España, *el almuerzo* es la comida más importante y substancial.  En los Estados Unidos, es *la cena*.  ¿A qué hora cenan ustedes en su casa?  ¿Cuánto tiempo pasan ustedes en la mesa?  ¿treinta minutos?  ¿dos horas?  ¿una hora?  ¿quince minutos?  ¿O es que ustedes no comen a la misma hora?

10.  ¿Cuál es mejor:  Comer la familia entera juntos, o comer separados?

11.  ¿Qué te gusta hacer los sábodos?  ¿practicar un deporte/ver la tele/hacer la tarea/preparar la cena/ir de compras/salir con los amigos/andar en bicicleta/monopatín, etc.?  ¿y los domingos?  ¿ir a la iglesia/la sinagoga/el templo?  ¿pasear por el parque o por el barrio?  ¿hacer un picnic?  ¿ir al cine?  ¿pasar la tarde con los abuelos?

# I. Gustar with indirect object pronouns

Learning how to use the verb *gustar* properly almost always causes initial difficulties for the beginning student, because it does not mean "to like" but rather "to please/be pleasing to".  This requires a reversal of subject and object:  Instead of the subject "I" liking something, in Spanish the "thing liked" is the subject, and is "pleasing to *me*. (me=the object)"  Let's look at the example:

*I*   *like*   *baseball*.       *Me*   *gusta*   *el béisbol*.
s     v     d.o.         ind.o.    v     s

And not only do you have to invert your thought process with *gustar* (switching subject and object), but the word order itself is also "backwards" to an English speaker:

*To me is pleasing the (game of) baseball.*

In English if you used pleasing, you would put the subject (baseball) first in the sentence ("Baseball is pleasing to me"); in Spanish, the subject comes at the end (Is pleasing to me baseball)!

If the above sounds complicated, don't worry.  It takes time to sink in.  <u>Fortunately, we can start with some simple exercises</u> that will get you "liking it" in no time.

By far the two most common types of gustar expressions involve either

1) <u>one thing</u> (singular) that pleases someone (*I like <u>it</u>*), or
2) <u>a number of things</u> (plural) that please someone (*I like <u>them</u>*).

To keep it simple, let's start with me, and what I like. I would say "Me gusta…el béisbol."  (For now, you can just remember that "me gusta" means "I like," if the above grammar has your head spinning).

You must also use "Me gusta…" when talking about not just a thing (like baseball), but an *activity* which uses a *verb infinitive*.

*Me gusta leer*.  I like to read.
*Me gusta dormir*.  I like to sleep.

For the exercises below, please refer to this table of indirect object pronouns:

INDIRECT OBJECT PRONOUNS

| **me**--*me* | **nos**--*us* |
|---|---|
| **te**--*you* (familiar: friend, sibling, close family member, pet* | **os**--*you guys you all you* (familiar plural) |
| **le**--*he, she, it you* (formal: stranger, pet*, authority figure, older person) | **les**--*them you* (formal plural) |

*Pets are usually familiar, but can be addressed in the formal if that is in the personality of the "pet guardian."  There is some delicious absurdity and just plain fun in addressing a pet using the formal "usted", such as "¿y a usted también le gusta este programa, Átlas?"

**A.** Translate to the Spanish:

1.  I like to eat.
    _Me gusta comer._

2.  I like the dog.
    _____

3.  I like (the) school.
    _____

4.  I like to sing.
    _____

5.  I like my new car.

    _____

PLURAL

Another way of saying "I like" in Spanish is "Me gusta**n**…"   The "-n" is necessary at the end because "more than one thing" is "pleasing to you," and since "more than one thing" is the subject driving the verb, the verb must be plural.  As you know,

    1 → 2 → 3       1 → 2 → 3
**They** speak Spanish.  Ellos hablan español.
   1 → 2 → 3   3 ← 2 ← 1
**They** please me.   Me gustan ellos.

Note that the English and Spanish read backwards to each other when using *gustar*.  You can check this by looking at the Spanish sentence, and start at the end, and read to the beginning, and it will sound like English:

*Me gustan los animales.*  I like (the) animals    (or)
(The) animals (they) please me.

Yes, this is hard at first.  It's hard for everyone.  It's like looking at an algebraic formula, and having to suddenly make constant use of it.  With continual use, however, it will "burn in" and you'll be proud of yourself when you finally do it.

**B.** Try these, putting them into Spanish:

1.  I like the books.
    _Me gustan los libros._
2.  I like the photos (las fotos).

    _____
3.  I like Ana and Luisa.

    _____
4.  I like the apples.

    _____

5.  I like the teachers (profesores).

_____

Corresponding to these pronouns are also the prepositional pronouns, which are grammatically *optional*, but used either for *emphasis* ("A mí me gusta el béisbol"), or for *clarification* when it is not clear who is referred to (this happens only in the <u>third person singular and plural</u>, because the same conjugation (say, *gusta*) is used for he, she, it, you (formal), them, and you (formal plural):  "A ella <u>le</u> gusta bailar," "A ellos <u>les</u> gusta cantar," etc.).

Here are the pronouns.  Note that they are identical to the subject pronouns (*yo, tú, él, ella*, etc.) except the first and second person singular*:

PREPOSITIONAL PRONOUNS

| SINGULAR | PLURAL |
|---|---|
| mí*--me | nosotros--us |
| ti*--you | vosotros--you |
| él--him | ellos--them |
| ella--her | ellas--them |
| usted--you | ustedes--you |

For comparison here are the SUBJECT PRONOUNS:

| SINGULAR | PLURAL |
|---|---|
| yo--I | nosotros--we |
| tú--you | vosotros--you |
| él--he | ellos--they |
| ella--she | ellas--they |
| usted--you | ustedes--you |

Now let's do something a little more challenging.  A shorthand way of understanding *gustar* if you only think of the above examples with *gusta* and *gustan*, is simply to keep in mind <u>if it is *one thing or activity* that you like (*gusta*), or *more than one thing* (*gustan*).</u> If you like it, and say so, you use "me" with "gusta".  If you *don't* like it, put the "no" in front:  "*No* me gusta…"

*Me          gusta          el helado.*
(To) me   is pleasing   the ice cream.   (literal translation)

I like ice cream.                                    (the way we say it)

If you tell, or ask, someone you are directly speaking with, about their likes or dislikes, you use "te" if they are a friend, or "le" if they are a stranger (exactly as you would use "tú" and "usted,").

¿*Te* gusta *(a ti)* el helado?      Do you like the ice cream?
¿*Le* gusta *(a usted)* el helado?   Do you like the ice cream?

If you are talking about *him* or *her*, or *it*, you also use "*le*":

| Español | Inglés | **Can also be said like this: |
|---|---|---|
| *Le gusta a ella bailar.* | She likes to dance. | *A ella le gusta bailar.* |
| *Le gusta a él cantar.* | He likes to sing. | *A él le gusta cantar.* |
| *Le gusta al perro ladrar.* | The dog likes to bark. | *Al perro le gusta ladrar.* |

Perhaps you see the pattern. The same works for "us" and "them" (or "you" plural):

*Nos gusta esta música.*           We like this music.
*Les gusta a los estudiantes hacer la tarea.*  The students like to do homework.
*Les gusta a ustedes ganar.*        You like to win (you team, group, etc.).

How would you re-write the sentence in the other way shown below (and just above)**?
Ejemplo:
Les gusta a los estudiantes hacer la tarea.   *A los estudiantes les gusta hacer la tarea.*

**C.** Ejercicio:
Siempre les gusta a ustedes ganar el partido.  _____

And of course there's the informal plural of *you guys*, which is in use in Spain only, that country of 43 million people, and corresponds to *vosotros*. In Mexico, the US, and Latin America the plural of *tú* is *ustedes* which technically is the *formal* form of you (the plural of *usted* of course); in Spain the original plural is maintained--*vosotros* for the subject pronoun *you*, and for the object pronoun *os* or *you*:

*A vosotros os gusta salir*    *por la noche*  *hasta*  *las tantas (horas de la mañana*).*
You guys like to go out    at night    until  the wee hours of the morning.
(*unspoken, but understood)

Of course all of the above examples, which only used the singular "gusta", could have had plural examples, using "gusta**n**". In "shorthand", if you like just one thing, use **gusta.** If more than one thing, use **gustan.** Por ejemplo:

*Me gustan los bailes.*
I like dances.

¿*Te gustan los bailes?*
Do** you like dances?

*Le gustan a ella los vestidos de la última moda.*
She likes dresses of the latest fashion.

*Le gustan a él los zapatos de la última moda.*
He likes shoes of the latest fashion.

*¿Le gustan a usted esos programas comerciales?*
Do** you like those commercial programs?

*Nos gustan los animales.*
We like animals.

*¿Os gustan a vosotros los experimentos sobre los animales, si eso ayuda salvar las vidas humanas?*
Do you like experiments on animals, if that helps to save human lives?

*Les gustan a ellos las computadoras.*
They like computers.

*Les gustan a ellas las vacaciones.*
They like vacations.

*Les gustan a ustedes la comida y la bebida de alta calidad.*
You like food and drink of the highest quality.
(Note that it's plural because of two singular items listed, la comida y la bebida; 1+1=2.)

**"Do" does not translate. In English "do" or "does" at the beginning of a sentence signals the beginning of a question; in Spanish, the tone of voice, or the context, indicates whether it is a question or a statement, or observation of fact or opinion.

## Proper nouns and nouns converted to Indirect Object Pronouns

When speaking of people (or things) it may not be immediately apparent which indirect object pronoun to use, nor where it goes in the sentence. For example, "Luisa likes the apples." Since "Luisa" is not in the above chart of indirect object pronouns, you have to realize that Luisa is a "her"—*ella,* and therefore *le.* That might not be too hard. But what about "el perro" (the dog)? What about "María y yo" (Mary and I)? Below is a master list that should be helpful.

| *me* / *a mí* | *nos* / *a nosotros/as* |
|---|---|
| (no other option) | a Juan y yo, a María y yo, a mis amigos y yo |
| *te* / *a ti* | *os* / *a vosotros/as* |
| (no other option) | a ti y tus amigos, a vuestros compañeros |
| *le* / *a ella:* | *les* / *a ellas:* |
| a Luisa | a Luisa y (a) Nuria |
| a la profesora | a las profesoras |
| a la mariposa | a las mariposas |
| (butterfly) | (butterflies) |
| *le* / *a él:* | *les* / *a ellos:* |
| a Paco | a Paco y (a) Luisa |

| | |
|---|---|
| al profesor | a los profesores |
| al gato | a los gatos |
| al Señor Gómez | a usted y (a) su(s) amigo(s) |
| al papel | a los papeles |

**Ejercicios con gustar (singular)**

**D.** The prepositional pronouns are given. With that information, you should be able to complete the sentences with the **indirect object pronouns**: *me, te, le, nos, os, les.*

1. ___*Le*___ gusta a Ana salir con las amigas.
2. _____ gusta a nosotros ir al cine.
3. _____ gusta a mi abuela ver la tele.
4. _____ gustan a mi hermana los chicos.
5. _____ gusta a ti cantar.
6. _____ gustan a vosotros la paella y los mariscos en general.
7. _____ gusta a mí estar en mi jardín.
8. _____ gusta al gato sentarse en el sillón, y meditar.
9. _____ gusta a Pablo y Juan pescar en el río, porque siempre vuelven a casa con muchos peces, y toda la familia come ese día.
10. _____ gustan a ustedes los bailes.

**E.** Complete the statements with logical answers. Use each answer only once, with the *best* answers for each. Note that only *one thing* or *activity* is liked, and therefore the singular *gusta* is used in all cases.

*A. cantar  B. dormir en el sofá  C. visitar con los nietos (grandchildren)*
*D. esperar por mucho tiempo  E. La Copa del Mundo  F.  vivir en paz    G. la paella*
*H.  estudiar  I. el agua  J. correr*

1. A la gente del mundo le gusta ___*vivir en paz*___
2. A las hormigas (ants) no les gusta _____
3. A los estudiantes responsables les gusta _____
4. A los niños no les gusta _____
5. A los atletas les gusta _____
6. A Cristina Aguilera le gusta _____
7. A los gatos les gusta _____
8. A los españoles les gusta preparar y comer _____
9. A los aficionados de fútbol les gusta _____
10. A los abuelos les gusta _____

**F.** Here are plural examples of *gustar*, where "more than one thing" is pleasing to the people who like them. Since there are more than one persons or things being liked, we use the plural "gusta<u>n</u>".

*A. los árboles B. el negocio (the business) de los armamentos y las guerras C. Ghandi y Martin Luther King D. las computadoras E. O (either) JesuCristo, o el Buda, o Mahoma, o Moises (u otras figuras), y Dios F. las zanohorias (carrots) G. las buenas notas (good grades) H. las pastas, la pizza y los espaguetis I. los jonrones J. el pastel y los dulces (sweets)*

1. A mi hermano, que siempre está en su cuarto, le gustan ___*las computadoras*___.
2. A los conejos les gustan _____
3. A los jugadores de béisbol les gustan _____ .
4. A los italianos les gustan _____ .
5. En la fiesta de cumpleaños, a los niños les gustan _____ .
6. A los estudiantes ambiciosos les gustan _____ .
7. A los pájaros les gustan _____ .
8. A los que creen en una religión, les gustan _____ .
9. A los pacifistas les gustan _____ .
10. A las compañías que fabrican armamentos, les gustan _____ .

**G. Open ended gustar questions (to be done orally, or written).**

1. ¿Te gustan los deportes?
_____

2. ¿Te gusta salir con tus amigos?
_____

3. ¿Te gusta escuchar la música clásica?
_____

4. ¿Te gusta trabajar?
_____

5. ¿Te gustan los videojuegos?
_____

6. ¿Le gusta a usted comer en un restaurante elegante si pagan los padres, o los amigos?
_____

7. ¿Le gustan a usted los programas de televisión, generalmente?
_____

8. ¿Les gusta a ustedes ganar en los deportes?
_____

9. ¿Les gusta a ustedes ganar dinero?
_____

10. Os gusta a vosotros estudiar las matemáticas?
_____

11. Os gusta a vosotros escuchar y hablar el español?
_____

# II. *También/Tampoco*

*También*--also, too
*Tampoco*--neither, either, nor

These are opposites. *También* is used to affirm, or second, an <u>affirmative</u> statement:
--Me gusta esta camisa.  --A mí también.
*I like this shirt.*          *Me too.*

*Tampoco* is used to affirm, or second, a <u>negative</u> statement:
--No me gusta esta camisa.  --A mí tampoco.
I don't like this shirt.          Me (n)either.

Note that if you *start* a sentence with *Tampoco*, you can't use "no" elsewhere.

*Tampoco quiero ir.*                                    (*Not:* Tampoco no quiero ir.)
Nor do I want to go.  (I don't want to go either.)

Some typical examples of *también* and *tampoco*:

*Me gusta esta película.   Sí, (a mí) también.   (A mí) también me gusta.*
Do you like this film?      Yeah, I do too.          I also like it.

*No me gusta esta película.   Tampoco.      Ni a mí tampoco.      A mí tampoco.*
*I don't like this film.*        *Me neither.*    *I don't either.*      *Nor do I.*

**A.** Fill in the blank with either *también* or *tampoco*.

1. --Me gusta la profesora Piñeda.  Es muy simpática e inteligente.
   --¿Sí?  A mí me gusta __*también*___ .
2. --Yo no voy a salir esta noche.
   --Yo _____ .
3. ¡Espera! _____ quiero lavarme las manos antes de comer.
4. A mí me gustan los cacahuetes _____ .
5. --Vamos al cine ahora.
   --¡Quiero ir _____!
6. --No me gusta el tabaco.
   --Ni a mí _____ .

# III. Definite articles ("the")

Since nouns in Spanish are either feminine or masculine*, there are two ways of saying "the" in the singular: *el* (masculine) and *la* (feminine).  And because Spanish requires that the definite article show singularity or plurality, its form must also change when the noun is plural: *los* (masculine plural) and *las* (feminine plural).  This presents a difficulty for the English-speaking learner of Spanish because in English we use the same "the" in *all cases*.  Here's how it looks graphically:

| DEF. ART. "the" | masculine | feminine |
|---|---|---|
| singular | *el* | *la* |
| plural | *los* | *las* |

*they are just that way owing to ancient times. There is not much "rhyme or reason" to it when one tries to figure out why some nouns are feminine and others masculine. Obviously, el muchacho and la muchacha would have to be the way they are; but why is a "sword" feminine ("la espada")? or "make-up/mascara" masculine ("el maquillaje")? Sometimes things are feminine or masculine for a reason, however: the moon ("la luna") is feminine, as is the earth ("la tierra"). And the sun, as well as the sky, is masculine ("el sol, el cielo"). To the ancients, this made perfect sense.

## Rules for identifying masculine and feminine nouns

The rule of thumb is that if it ends in an -*a*, it's feminine, but if it ends in an -*o*, it's masculine. And if it ends in an -*e* or a *consonant (-d, -l, -j, -n, -r, -s, -y, or -z)*, <u>you'll just have to remember</u> its gender the next time by noting whether it had a masculine or feminine article attached to it.

This rule of thumb, at the beginning level, works pretty well:

*<u>la</u> muchacha*--the girl
*<u>la</u> casa*--the house
*<u>la</u> mesa*--the table
*<u>la</u> vida*--the life

*<u>el</u> muchacho*--the boy
*<u>el</u> carro*--the car (Latin America); the cart (Spain)
*<u>el</u> ojo*--the eye
*<u>el</u> pescado*--the fish

However, there are a few <u>exceptions</u> at the beginning level to be aware of. The following are <u>not feminine</u>:

el map<u>a</u>--the map
el dí<u>a</u>**--the day
el planet<u>a</u>--the planet
el poem<u>a</u>*--the poem
el program<u>a</u>*--the program

*all words of Greek origin that end in -ma, -ema or -ama are masculine, unless when two words sound so similar that for a slightly hearing-impaired person there might be a problem, such as with *<u>la</u> trama* (the plot) and *<u>el</u> drama* (the play itself), since the "tr-" and the "dr-" are almost identical in a noisy room. This distinguishing evolutionary tactic was also used for *<u>la</u> fuente* (the fountain) and *<u>el</u> puente* (the bridge), since "p-" and "f-" also sound similar in a crowded noisy room (try saying *puente* and *fuente* with "la"in front of each, out loud to yourself. If you live with older people who are hard of hearing, or with people whose hearing is hard because they hardly hear, then you will probably understand the need for the definite articles being different in front of each).
**Perhaps this is why *día* is masculine, since *tía (aunt)* is feminine.

Not masculine:
la man<u>o</u>
la mot<u>o</u>***
la fot<u>o</u>***

***La mano* is a genuine exception. *La moto* and *la foto* are not, since *moto* and *foto* are the shortened colloquial versions of *motociclet<u>a</u>* and *fotograf<u>í</u>a*, which are feminine according to the rules.

**A.** Write in either *el, la, los,* or *las.*

1. _*La*_ madre de tu madre es tu abuela.
2. En _____ semana hay siete días.
3. _____ días que me gustan más son sábado y domingo.
4. Por fin el hombre dice, --Necesitamos _____ mapa porque no sé dónde estamos.
5. En _____ casa hay tres dormitorios, una cocina, una sala de estar, y dos baños.
6. _____ frutas que producimos aquí son _____ bananas y _____ mangos.
7. ¡Vamos! Pepe y Conchita nos esperan en _____ carro.
8. A la gente no le gusta _____ guerra, pero en _____ historia hay muchas, una tras otra.
9. _____ hombres son de Martes, y _____ mujeres son de Venus.
10. Nos dice el guía que _____ aguas de este río curan cualquier enfermedad.
11. Ricardo toca _____ batería, Pablo toca _____ bajo, Juan toca _____ guitarra, y Jorge también toca _____ guitarra.
12. _____ ventanas de mi casa están abiertas para dejar entrar el aire y el sol.

Other basic vocabulary words that end in vowels or consonants are:
*la clase*--the class  *el papel*--the paper  *el hombre*--the man  *la mujer*--the woman
*el mar*--the sea  *el reloj*--the clock/watch  *el país*--the country  *el bienestar*--well-being
*el coche*--the car  *el tren*--the train  *el arroz*--the rice  *el olor*--the smell  *la paz*--(the) peace  *la luz*-the light  *la red*--the net/the Internet  *el estrés*--stress  *la ley*--the law

**B.** Fill in the sentences so that they make sense, using one of the words above, each word once only. Write also "el" or "la", except in #2.

1. Un plato típico de comida en el campo incluye los vegetales, los frijoles, y _*el arroz.*_
2. --¿Qué hora es?
   --Según mi _____, son las dos.
3. Ese galeón español, con todo su oro, y con los esqueletos de los marineros, hasta hoy se encuentra en _____ .
4. Para mí, _____ de álgebra es la más difícil.
5. A veces, _____ y (6) _____ se enamoran a primera vista.
7. _____ es más que la ausencia de la violencia.

8. En _____ hay mucha información. Alguna información encontrada allí es verdad, mucha es pura opinión, y alguna es descarada mentira.

9. ¿Cuál es _____ más seguro: el que tiene cuatro llantas o tres?

10. -- _____ de tu perfume me vuelve loco, Griselda.

11. _____ del estado requiere que se laven las manos después de usar el retrete, si usted trabaja en un restaurante.

12. Voy a tomar _____ para Segovia a las siete horas de la mañana.

13. Estoy listo. Tengo aquí mis libros, el cuaderno, el bolígrafo, y _____ .

14. Las personas que no saben relajarse sufren _____ .

15. Es más importante _____ que el dinero.

16. _____ es respetado más por sus valores económicos que por su fuerza militar.

17. En la oscuridad es difícil ver; hay que encender _____ para ver.

# IV. Nouns that end in *-ón*

The suffix *-ón* is often an augmentative, meaning that it makes the original noun "bigger" or "more". Many words also simply end in *-ón*. Perhaps 98% of them are masculine nouns. An exception, of concern to beginning students, is <u>la razón</u>, which is "reason" or "being right" when used with *tener*: *Tienes razón* ("You're right").

**A.** Use each of the following words once. FEMININE: *razón*--reason
MASCULINE: *limón*--lemon  *montón*--a lot  *melón*--melon  *barrigón*--pot belly, paunch  *campeón*--champion  *ladrón*--thief  *jamón*--ham  *sabón*--soap  *corazón*--heart

1. Antes de comer, es buena idea lavarse las manos, usando el _____ .

2. Miguel es muy simpático; tiene un _____ de oro.

3. En el fútbol, Brasil es el _____ del mundo, y con mucha frecuencia.

4. No tenemos que discutir más. Oigo lo que dice usted, y me parece que usted tiene _____ . No sé por qué no comprendí la verdad antes de escuchar sus ideas.

5. El _____ es la carne del cerdo, del puerco.

6. El _____ les roba a las personas.

7. El _____ es una fruta amarilla.

8. El _____ es una de las frutas mas sabrosas y saludables.

9. Cuando alguien llega a tener los 50 años, es posible encontrarse con _____ si se vive una vida ante la tele y se come y se bebe comida y bebida no saludable.

10. Tengo un _____ de trabajo que hacer esta noche.

## V. Hyperbaton (word order for poetic purposes)

To make poems rhyme, word order is sometimes conveniently re-arranged, and the result is that what is said or written ends up not sounding conversational. This is called *hyperbaton*, when it is done for poetic or lyrical reasons.  Góngora was the Spanish poet who is perhaps most associated with this practice (to such an extreme in his case that it became an end in itself).  In my case, for these songs, it was simply out of necessity, to get the rhyme!

An example in the song where the word order (syntax) has been changed to allow for a rhyme would be the following:

*A mi amiga le gusta*
*al golf y al béisbol*
*y al tenis jugar*
*a ella le gusta pintar*
*a ella le gusta viajar*

"Jugar," when speaking conversationally, should go in the following place:

*A mi amiga le gusta jugar*
*al golf y al béisbol*            ← (and you'd drop the 'y' here)
*y al tenis ____X____ ↑*
*A ella le gusta pintar*
*A ella le gusta viajar*

because normally the infinitive (*jugar*) immediately follows the conjugated form of *gustar*.

**A.** In the following verses in the song, identify (by circling) the word that is "poetically" out of place, and then put it in its more correct and conversational place, by drawing an arrow to between the words where it belongs.

1.  *A mis primos les gusta*
*montar a caballo*
*y animales criar*
*Les gusta vivir en el campo*
*Les gusta el aire tomar*

2.  *A nosotros nos gusta*
*a la familia entera*
*a las dos almorzar*
*Nos gusta en casa estar*
*Nos gusta también conversar*

# 5. Amañamo

<u>Idiomatic expressions to learn before hearing the song</u>:
*a lo lejos* -- at a distance, from far away
*me muero por ti* -- I'm dying for you
*hacer el favor* -- to do the favor (of)...

Veo como sonríes y te conozco
Oigo como _____ y tu ser yo adivino
Observo como andas  y me _____
Yo sé como te sientes aunque te miro a lo lejos

Sin saber tu _____
Estoy enamorado
_____ yo me siento
No puedo remediarlo
_____ encantarte
Te quiero cautivar

_____ decirte que te amo
Y mágicamente te programo
_____ decirte que te amo
Y mágicamente te programo

Te digo que yo salgo  con mi _____
Te pongo en las _____ el corazón de pecador
Te traigo unas flores perfumadas
Te hago el_____...de declararte el amor
De declararte el amor
De declararte el amor
De declararte el amor

—

Sin saber tu _____
Estoy enamorado
_____ yo me siento
No puedo remediarlo
_____ encantarte
Te quiero cautivar

_____ decirte que te amo
Y mágicamente te programo
_____ decirte que te amo
Y mágicamente te programo

Veo como sonríes y te conozco
Oigo como _____ y tu ser yo adivino
Observo como andas y me _____
Yo sé como te sientes aunque te miro a lo lejos

Sin saber tu _____
Estoy enamorado
_____ yo me siento
No puedo remediarlo
_____ encantarte
Te quiero cautivar

_____ decirte que te amo
Y mágicamente te programo
¿Cuál es el nombre que te llamo?
Sin saberlo te llamo "Amañamo"
En secreto, digo "Amañamo"
Te quiero tanto, "Amañamo"
Me muero por_____, "Amañamo"

Copyright Tom Blodget February 18, 2003

## El Banco de Palabras:
These are the words that are missing in the song:

favor   gusta   hablas   madre   manos   mejor   nombre   quiero   ti   así

# Vocabulario

Below are the words and phrases of the song in English, in the order of their appearance in the song.  Fill in quickly as much of the Spanish as you know, without looking up any words in the dictionary or glossary.  Any words or phrases that you *don't* know, which are "sandwiched" between words you *do* know, may be confidently identified by deduction.  This method eliminates the need for a dictionary.

| | |
|---|---|
| _____ | I see |
| _____ | how you smile |
| _____ | and I know you |
| _____ | I hear |
| _____ | how you talk |
| _____ | and your being I divine |
| _____ | I observe |
| _____ | how you walk |
| _____ | and I like it |
| _____ | I know |

| | |
|---|---|
| _____ | how you feel |
| _____ | although |
| _____ | I watch you |
| _____ | from afar ("at a distance") |
| _____ | Without knowing |
| _____ | your name |
| _____ | I am in love ("enamored") |
| _____ | this way |
| _____ | I feel |
| _____ | I can't help it ("remedy" it) |
| _____ | I want to charm you |
| _____ | You |
| _____ | I want |
| _____ | to capture/captivate |
| _____ | (It's probably) better |
| _____ | to tell you |
| _____ | that you I love |
| _____ | and magically |
| _____ | I'll program you |

…(repeat)

| | |
|---|---|
| _____ | I tell you |
| _____ | that I go out |
| _____ | with my mom |
| _____ | I put in your hands ("the" hands) |
| _____ | the heart |
| _____ | of the |
| _____ | sinner |
| _____ | I bring you |
| _____ | some flowers |
| _____ | perfumed |
| _____ | I do you the favor |
| _____ | of declaring my love for you (4x) |

…(repeat chorus)
…(repeat first verse)
…(repeat chorus)

| | |
|---|---|
| _____ | what is the name |
| _____ | that I call you? |
| _____ | without |
| _____ | knowing it |
| _____ | I call you "Amañamo" |
| _____ | In secret I say "Amañamo" |
| _____ | I want you so much "Amañamo" |
| _____ | I am dying |
| _____ | for you, "Amañamo" |

## Preguntas Orales.

These questions are to check for comprehension, and should be asked orally after listening to the song several times with the above activities.

1.  Este hombre, ¿es muy buen amigo de esa mujer (sí o no)? ¿La conoce bien (sí o no)? ¿O para él, es ella una fantasía, un sueño, una persona a quién NO conoce (sí o no)?

2.  ¿Por qué el hombre no sabe el nombre de esa mujer--¿Es porque no son amigos, ni conocidos (sí o no)?

3.  ¿Le gusta al hombre esa mujer? (¿Sí o no? ¿Tal vez?) ¿Y el contrario? ¿Le gusta a esa mujer este hombre? (Sí o no?)

4.  ¿Creen ustedes que esa mujer conoce a este hombre apasionado? (¿Sí o no?) (¿Tal vez?)

## I. *(Yo) -go* **irregular verbs** *(oír--to hear; salir--to leave, to date; poner--to put/to set; hacer--to do/to make; traer--to bring; decir--to say/to tell; plus veo from ver--to see.)*

This song uses all seven (7) of these slightly irregular and very important verbs normally taught together in most texts, six of which have the hard 'g' sound inserted in the last syllable of the *yo* form: *oigo, salgo, pongo, hago, traigo, and digo.*

The first five verbs are otherwise conjugated as regular verbs, plus *traer--traer* has an extra *'i'* inserted in the *'yo'* form ("yo traigo") because if not, it would be *trago*, which is the *yo* form of *tragar*, which means "to swallow" or "to gulp."

*Decir* is an *e_i* stem-changing verb. Stem-changing verbs (see "Te Quiero Como Eres") suffer conjugational distortion in "the boot" part of the table (you would expect it--*were it regular*--to be d**e**co, d**e**ces, d**e**ce, decimos, decís, d**e**cen):

| digo | decimos |
|------|---------|
| dices | decís |
| dice | dicen |

So by taking the '-g' in the *yo* form, it is *doubly* irregular.

The verb *ver* ("to see") would expectedly be conjugated *"yo vo,"* but the 'e' was probably kept in *("yo veo")* to maintain the character or identity of the infinitive.

**A.** Make the following sentences correct with your completion, using any of the above verbs in the 'yo' form. You may use them more than once, or not at all.

*oigo   salgo   pongo   hago   traigo   digo   veo*

1. Yo nunca __*hago*__ la cama por la mañana, porque tengo que salir de la casa rápido.
2. Ahora vengo. Te _____ tus gafas.
3. Yo siempre _____ de la casa a las siete y media de la mañana.
4. Habla más despacio, por favor, y en voz alta. No te _____ bien.
5. Cuando entro en la sala de clase, siempre le _____ al profesor "Buenos días."
6. En mi casa, mi madre prepara la comida, yo _____ la mesa, y mi padre lava los platos.
7. Yo no _____ ninguna posibilidad de aprobar (pasar) este examen. Es muy difícil. Y yo nunca (8) _____ la tarea.
9. _____ el ruido en la calle; hay mucho tráfico. Prefiero otra habitación.
10. Ahora _____ con mi futura esposa.

## II. *Saber/Conocer*

These two verbs both mean "to know." Like with *ser* and *estar*, you have to know when to use which one. They both conjugate as regular verbs, **except** the *yo* form:

CONOCER--to know (intimately or personally--people, places, or things); to meet (people):

| conozco | conocemos |
|---------|-----------|
| conoces | conocéis  |
| conoce  | conocen   |

SABER-- to know facts; to know of/about someone or something; to know "how to" do something:

| sé    | sabemos |
|-------|---------|
| sabes | sabéis  |
| sabe  | saben   |

Note these usages:

### CONOCER--to know, to meet

1. to know someone
*Sí, yo* **conozco** *a Rosana Soler. Su familia tiene una tienda en la Costa Blanca, cerca de la playa, en Jávea.*
Yes, I know Rosana Soler. Her family has a store on the *Costa Blanca*, near the beach, in Jávea.

2. to meet someone
**Conozco** *a muchas personas vivas e interesantes en mi profesión.*

I meet many vivacious and interesting people in my profession.

<u>3.  to know a place</u>
*Yo **conozco** Madrid como **conozco** mi propia casa.*
I know Madrid like I know my own house.

<u>4.  to know a thing</u>
*--¿**Conoces** este libro?*
*--Sí, lo **conozco**. Es la primera novela.  Cervantes es el autor.  Es buen libro.  Vale la pena leer.  Es un gran comentario sobre la condición del ser humano, y además, es muy gracioso.*
"Do you know this book?"
"Yes, I know it.  It's the first novel.  Cervantes is the author.  It's a good book.  It's worth reading.  It's a brilliant commentary on the human condition, and besides, it's quite funny."

### SABER--to know

<u>5.  to know facts</u>
*Yo **sé** que Don Quijote fue la primera novela.*
I know that *Don Quijote* was the first novel.

<u>6.  to know "how to" do something</u>
*También yo **sé nadar**.  Siempre voy a Jávea por un mes, todos los veranos, y nado en el mar, ceno en los restaurantes, y conozco a mucha gente.*
I also know how to swim.  I always go to Jávea for a month, every summer, and I swim in the ocean, eat dinner in the restaurants, and meet a lot of people.

<u>7.  to know about someone</u>
*Yo no conozco a Rosana, pero **sé** de ella.*
*Dicen que es casada, con tres hijos, y ya es la dueña de esa tienda, porque sus padres ya se han jubilado.*
I don't know Rosana, but I know about her.
They say that she's married, with three kids, and now is the owner of that store, because her parents have now retired.

**A.** Write *sé* or *conozco* in the blanks, and also indicate in parentheses
(1) through (7) from above, to indicate **why** you chose *saber* or *conocer*.

1.  Yo ___*sé (6)*__ jugar al básquetbol.
2.  Yo no _____ a ningún Pepito Pícaro.  Él no vive aquí.
3.  Yo no _____ esta ciudad.  Por favor, ¿me puede decir dónde está un restaurante económico?
4.  Sí, yo _____ que ese restaurante es *bueno, barato, y bonito*, porque el hijo del zapatero almuerza allí de vez en cuando, y le dice a su padre que lo es, y el padre mi colega me dice lo mismo.

5. Hay uno en la esquina allí. (Yo) lo _____ bien, porque ceno allí cada semana. Es *excelente, económico, y elegante.*

6. --Hijo, ¡usted está solo! ¿Va a comer solo?

    --Acabo de llegar a Madrid. (Yo) no _____ a nadie. Me gusta ir a los restaurantes y hablar con los clientes. De esta manera (7.) _____ a la gente.

## III. *Poder/Querer/Deber* + Infinitive

This concept is commonly used but not often studied formally. The first verb is conjugated, but the second one is left in its infinitive form. A common error is to conjugate both verbs, as in *quiero voy (I want I go),* instead of *quiero ir (I want to go).*

*Puedo ir. Quiero ir. Debo ir.*
I can go. I want to go. I must go.

Also making understanding difficult is the fact that in English the "to" is omitted in the first and third sentences, obscuring the fact that it is an infinitive. Of course, *Puedo ir* can also be translated into the less common "I am able **to** go." And because the infinitive form of all verbs in English require the word "to", one often hears Spanish speaking learners of English say incorrectly, "I must **to** go," or "I can **to** go." They are making the understandable mistake of translating *literally* from Spanish to English.

QUERER--to want

| quiero | queremos |
|--------|----------|
| quieres | queréis |
| quiere | quieren |

PODER--can, to be able

| puedo | podemos |
|-------|---------|
| puedes | podéis |
| puede | pueden |

DEBER--must, should, to owe

| debo | debemos |
|------|---------|
| debes | debéis |
| debe | deben |

**A.** In the following sentences you have to do two things: 1) decide whether to use *querer, poder,* or *deber* (the *best* choice), and 2) conjugate that verb correctly in the blank.

1. Todos los ciudadanos _*deben*_ obedecer las leyes.
2. Claudio _____ casarse con Isabel; está enamorado de ella. Son novios.

3. ¿_____ (yo) usar tu computadora?  Quiero buscar algo en la red (el Internet).

4. (Nosotros) no _____ entrar; el restaurante está cerrado.

5. ¿Saben ustedes dónde están las llaves?  Yo no las _____ encontrar.

6. _____ (yo) ir a casa ahora.  Ya es muy tarde.  Mis padres me van a castigar (punish).

7. _____ (tú) escribirme con más frecuencia.  Si no me escribes, voy a pensar que estás muerta.

8. ¿_____ (vosotros) ir al centro?  Ya comienza el concierto en la plaza.

9. --¡Mamá!  ¡Mírame, _____ andar en bicicleta sin caerme!

10. (Yo) no _____ asistir a la escuela hoy.  Tengo dos exámenes.

## IV. *Sin/Con* (without/with)

These words work just as they do in English, yet please note that *sin* is often followed by a verb infinitive, in the song:

*Sin **saber** tu nombre, estoy enamorado...*
Without **knowing** your name, I am in love…

In such a case the verb infinitive translates as a gerund ("knowing").

**A.** Write *sin* or *con* in the blanks.

1. --¿Quiere usted las papas fritas _con_ la hamburguesa?
2. A los españoles les gusta el café _____ leche.
3. Yo nunca salgo a la calle _____ ponerme la ropa.
4. Firmar un documento legal _____ leerlo es estúpido.
5. África es un continente _____ muchos problemas económicos.

## V. Placement of Direct and Indirect Object Pronouns with Infinitives and with the Present Progressive Tense

The direct object pronouns (*me, te, lo, la, nos, os, los, las*) or indirect object pronouns (*me, te, le, nos, os, les*) may immediately *precede* a compound verb structure, or they may be *attached* to the infinitive or present participle *(-iendo/-ando)* at the end.  Note the examples:

**Direct object:**

*Quiero encantar**te**.*
***Te** quiero encantar.*

(I want to charm you.)

*Me estás tomando el pelo.*
*Estás tomándome\* el pelo.*

(You are kidding me.)

### Indirect object:

*Quiero declararle el amor (a usted).*
*Le quiero declarar el amor (a usted).*

(I want to declare my love for you.)

*Le estoy enviando una carta.*
*Estoy enviándole\* una carta.*

(I'm sending you a letter.)

Both usages are common, and neither usage changes the meaning one iota, nor does it indicate where you're from or what dialect you speak.  Just as it's up to you how you pronounce the words "neither" (_ or _, "neether/nigh-ther") or "garage" ('garazhe' or 'garadge') without anyone taking conscious notice (at least in California!), or whether you say "Me either" or "Me neither"); so it is with the placement of these pronouns.

**A.** Re-write the sentences so that the pronouns are in the "alternate" place\*.  Remember if you attach a pronoun at the end of the present participle *(-ing* form of the verb: *-iendo/-ando*), you need to place the accent on the third to last syllable.

1.  **Me** estoy comiendo el coco.  (slang in Spain: el coco=la cabeza.  It means "to worry")
    _*Estoy comiéndome el coco.*_____
2.  Estás haciéndome un gran favor.
    _____
3.  Estoy esperándote aquí.
    _____
4.  No te estoy entendiendo.
    _____
5.  Me estás volviendo loco.
    _____

## 6. Te quiero como eres

Idiomatic expressions to learn before hearing the song:
*Me doy cuenta* -- I realize (suddenly or eventually), from *darse cuenta*
*luego que* -- as soon as
*así que* -- so, therefore

A ti  te quiero _____ eres
Y a mí  me gustaría conocerte mejor
Tu _____ me ilumina
Y la idea de _____ contigo me domina

Luego que yo veo tu faz
Me entra una _____ paz
Me doy cuenta de que soy capaz
De _____

Es cierto que siempre nos frecuentamos
_____ obvio que nos amamos
Sería un pecado no decir _____
  Hablamos del asunto
  Así que te pregunto
¿Quisieras comprometerte _____ conmigo?


–

A mí, ¿me quieres como_____?
A ti, te agradezco por lo _____que estoy
Tu _____ me ilumina
Y la idea de _____ contigo me domina

La verdad _____ miente
El amor siempre siente
su pareja _____el Puente de Amor

Nunca voy a abandonarte, no
Siempre te seré fiel
Sería un pecado no decir_____
  Hablamos del asunto
  Así que te pregunto
¿Quisieras comprometerte _____ conmigo?


Copyright Tom Blodget 1995, 2003

<u>El Banco de Palabras:</u>
These are the words that are missing in the song:

amar  belleza   como   dulce  en  es  estar   feliz  nada  nunca  soy  tú

# Vocabulario

Below are the words and phrases of the song in English, in the order of their appearance in the song.  Fill in quickly as much of the Spanish as you know, without looking up any words in the dictionary or glossary.  Any words or phrases that you *don't* know, which are "sandwiched" between words you *do* know, may be confidently identified by deduction.  This method eliminates the need for a dictionary.

| | |
|---|---|
| _____ | I want (love) you |
| _____ | as you are |
| _____ | and I would like |
| _____ | to know you better |
| _____ | your beauty |
| _____ | illuminates me |
| _____ | and the idea of |
| _____ | being with you |
| _____ | dominates/obsesses me |
| _____ | as soon as |
| _____ | I see your countenance/face |
| _____ | enters into me |
| _____ | a sweet peace |
| _____ | I realize |
| _____ | I am capable |
| _____ | of loving |
| _____ | It's true |
| _____ | that always |
| _____ | we see each other |
| _____ | It's obvious |
| _____ | that we love each other |
| _____ | It would be a sin |
| _____ | not to say anything* |
| _____ | We shall speak on this issue* |
| _____ | (and) So/therefore |
| _____ | I ask you |
| _____ | Would you like |
| _____ | to get engaged |
| _____ | to me? |
| _____ | Do you love me |
| _____ | as I am? |
| _____ | I am grateful to you |
| _____ | for how happy I am |

_____Your beauty
_____lights me up
_____and the idea of being with you
_____controls me
_____the truth
_____never
_____lies
_____love
_____always
_____senses
_____its mate
_____on the Bridge of Love
_____never
_____am I going to
_____leave you, no
_____always
_____will I be faithful
…(repeat ending: _it would be a sin…_)

## Preguntas Orales.

These questions are to check for comprehension, and should be asked orally after listening to the song several times with the above activities.

1. ¿Quiere cambiar a la chica, o le gusta tal come es?

2. ¿Son novios, o es una idea de él?

3. ¿Son amigos (sí o no)?

4. ¿Cómo sabes que ya son amigos?

5. ¿Es introvertido o extrovertido él?

6. ¿Le será fiel a ella (sí o no)? ¿o tiene la idea de tener tres o cuatro novias durante el mismo año (sí o no)?

7. Según el chico, ¿es fea la chica, o guapa?

# I. Direct and Indirect Object Pronouns

The **indirect object** indicates _to whom_ or _for whom_ (or _to/for what_) something is being done. The **direct object** indicates _who_ or _what_ receives the action of the verb, directly. (It is not easy to study the one without the other, since many sentences have both.) The archetypal sentence in English using both objects would be as follows:

*I give the ball to Pablo.*
I give what? *I give the ball.* The ball is the <u>direct object</u>, "what"?
To whom (or for whom…) do I give the ball?
*To Pablo.* Pablo is therefore the <u>indirect object</u>.

So what are the pronouns? The pronouns substitute for the object itself, so that you don't have to keep repeating the person's name, or the object, again and again:

I give the ball to Pablo. I give it to him.

"It" is the ball (direct object), and "him" is Pablo (the indirect object).

Here are the charts in both Spanish and English of both the Direct and Indirect Object Pronouns:

## INDIRECT OBJECT PRONOUNS

| me--me | nos--us |
|---|---|
| te--you (familiar) | os--you (familiar plural) |
| le--him, her, it, or you (formal) | les--them, you (formal plural) |

Note that there *is no* masculine or feminine distinction; the pronouns may represent either masculine or feminine things or people.

The direct object pronouns are the same, except in the 3rd person, where the masculine and feminine pronouns cause a subdivision:

## DIRECT OBJECT PRONOUNS

| me--me | nos--us |
|---|---|
| te--you (familiar) | os--you (familiar plural) |
| lo (m.)--him, her, it, or you (formal) | los--them, you (formal plural) |
| la (f.)--him, her, it, or you (formal) | las--them, you (formal plural) |

Note the masculine and feminine distinction in the 3rd person. Note also that among native Spanish speakers, depending on region and dialect, the *le* and the *lo/la*, or the *les* and the *los/las*, may be switched. For example, in "*le*-ismo", *le(s)* is used instead of *lo(s)/la(s)*. <u>The charts above are the correct, standard, and most widely-observed usages in the Spanish-speaking world.</u> As with everything else, feel free to "speak in dialect," but only after you have understood the master template upon which such variations are based.

Note these sentences, as examples of the above.

## INDIRECT OBJECT PRONOUNS
Me das un regalo. *You give me a present.*
Te doy un regalo. *I give you a present.*
Le doy a Pepe un regalo. *I give him a present.*
Le doy a Josefa un regalo. *I give her a present.*

Le doy a usted un regalo. *I give you a present.*
Nos doy a nosotros un regalo. *I give us a present.*
Os doy a vosotros un regalo. *I give you all a present.*
Les doy a Eduardo y Felipe un regalo. *I give them a present.*
Les doy a Ana y Silvia un regalo. *I give them a present.*
Les doy a ustedes un regalo. *I give you a present.*

DIRECT OBJECT PRONOUNS
Me ves. *You see me.*
Te veo. *I see you.*
Lo veo (a Juan). *I see him.*
La veo (a Ana). *I see her.*
Lo veo (a usted). *I see you (a male).*
La veo (a usted). *I see you (a female).*
Lo veo (el coche). *I see it.*
La veo (la casa). *I see it.*
Nos veo. *I see us.*
Os veo. *I see y'all.*
Los veo (a los estudiantes). *I see them.*
Las veo (a las profesoras). *I see them.*
Los veo (los coches). *I see them.*
Las veo (las casas). *I see them.*
Los veo (a ustedes). *I see you (male or m./f. mix).*
Las veo (a ustedes). *I see you (female group).*

Studying the above examples should help you in the exercises below.

Note the major difference with the pronouns between English and Spanish (besides the placement of the pronouns--*see below*) is the redundant use of the indirect object and its corresponding pronoun.

Here is the sentence in Spanish:

*Le*      *doy*   **la pelota**   *a Pablo.*
*(to) him I give the ball to Pablo. (literal translation)*

"Le" is the indirect object pronoun, and "a Pablo" is the indirect object itself ("to whom"). "La pelota" is *what* is being given, so it is the direct object.

The pronoun *Le* is mandatory in this sentence (unlike in English). You cannot say:

*Doy la pelota a Pablo.* (wrong)
I give the ball to Pablo.

You can omit the indirect object itself ("Pablo"), however, if it is already understood that we're talking about him ("Pablo").

*Le        doy     la pelota.*
Him        I give   the ball (to).

**A.** Translate the following sentences to Spanish, omitting people's names (proper nouns) and subject pronouns (*Yo, tú, nosotros*, etc.):

1.  I give my love to Esperanza.
    *Le doy mi amor*_____
2.  They tell the news to Lucía.
    _____
3.  I serve the salad to Mr. and Mrs. Villarreal.
    _____
4.  We prepare the food for the kids.
    _____
5.  Y'all sing me pretty songs.
    _____

## Placement of pronouns

**Note the placement of the direct object pronoun.** In Spanish, it appears directly *before* a conjugated verb. In English, it appears *after*:

(Before, in Spanish): ***Te*** *quiero.*     (After, in English): *I want **you**.*

**B.** Re-write the sentences, <u>converting the direct object into a pronoun</u> and placing it <u>in front of the conjugated verb</u>:

1. No saben la verdad.
   *No la saben.*_____
2. Él ve la casa.
   _____
3. Ella lava el coche.
   _____
4. Yo como la manzana.
   _____
5. Nosotros tomamos la leche.
   _____

### Note the placement of the indirect object pronoun:

***Te*** *pregunto si tienes un dólar, porque necesito gasolina para mi coche.*
*I ask **you** if you have a dollar, because I need gasoline for my car.*

<u>Rule, therefore:</u> *If only one object pronoun is used in a simple present tense sentence, it must immediately precede (go in front of) the conjugated verb.* {In other words, you <u>can't</u> say "Quiérote." (*I want you.*)}

**C.** Fill in the <u>indirect object pronoun</u> (*me, te, le, nos, os, les*) indicated by the prepositional pronoun or proper noun in the sentence:

1.  A nosotros Diego __*nos*_____ dice que podemos ir con él a la playa mañana.
2.  A mí _____ gusta la idea.
3.  A ellos Diego _____ va a llevar al hotel, pero después, tienen que caminar a la playa.
4.  A ellas _____ va a llevar directamente a la playa.
5.  A ti ¿qué _____ parece eso?

**Note the placement of the pronouns when used with the infininitive (not conjugated), in this case with the "*ir* + '*a*' + *infinitive*" structure:**

DIRECT OBJECT PRONOUN:
1. Nunca voy a abandonar**te**.
2. Nunca **te** voy a abandonar.
*I will never leave you.*

INDIRECT OBJECT PRONOUN
1.  Va a dominar**me** la idea de estar contigo
2.  **Me** va a dominar la idea de estar contigo
*The idea of being with you is going to obsess **me**.*

**Note when used with the present progressive tense (*estar* + *-ando/-iendo*):**

DIRECT OBJECT PRONOUN
1.  No estoy abandonándo**te**.
2.  No **te** estoy abandonando.
*I am not leaving **you**.*

INDIRECT OBJECT PRONOUN
1.  Está dominándo**me** la idea de estar contigo.
2.  **Me** está dominando la idea de estar contigo.
*The idea of being with you is obsessing **me**.*

<u>Rule:</u> *In all cases the pronoun can be "attached" to the end of the infinitive or gerund (1), or placed directly in front of the conjugated compound verb (2).*
Note that the *-ándo* or *-iéndo* requires the accent mark if the pronoun is *attached* at the end.

**D.** Place the indirect object pronoun immediately before the verb structure in these examples:

1.  A usted __*le*___ va a gustar mucho.

2. A ti no _____ va a importar en absoluto (*at all*).
3. A mi hermana _____ está costando mucho dinero los gastos de su hija.
4. A vosotros _____ va a encantar esta verbena.
5. A ustedes no _____ estamos engañando.

## How to form the pronouns from the objects

We do it in English all the time, so we will use that example first.

I ate <u>the burrito</u>.
I ate <u>it</u>.

If you peruse the above object pronoun charts, you can get a pretty good idea. A problem arises when you are confronted with how to convert "los estudiantes," "el Señor Gómez," "Esteban y yo," "ustedes y su ejército," "vosotros y vuestra pandilla," *etcetera,* into the corresponding pronouns. (This problem also presents itself to the beginning student when conjugating verbs.) Below is a chart with as many of these noun combinations as possible, which will often require "pro-nouning". The pronouns in *italics* are what you would use in each case (e.g. "a <u>María</u> y yo" = *nos/a nosotr<u>as</u>*).*

| *me / a mí* | *nos / a nosotros/as* |
|---|---|
| (no other option) | a Juan y yo, a María y yo, a mis amigos y yo |
| *te / a ti* | *os / a vosotros/as* |
| (no other option) | a ti y tus amigos, a vuestros compañeros |
| *le (indirect) la (direct) / a ella:* | *les (indirect) las (direct) / a ellas:* |
| a Emilia | a Emilia y (a) Nuria |
| a la profesora | a las profesoras |
| *le (indirect); lo (direct) / a él:* | *les (indirect); los (direct) / a ellos:* |
| a Paco | a Paco y (a) Emilia |
| al profesor | a los profesores |
| al gato | a los gatos |
| al Señor Gómez | a usted y (a) sus amigos |
| al papel | a los papeles |

*Note also that the prepostion "para" is also often used with the indirect object; "a" is the most common.

**E.** Re-write the sentences, converting the noun or proper noun to its corresponding <u>direct object pronoun</u>. Because the verb is in the simple <u>present tense</u>, you must place the pronoun directly <u>before</u> the conjugated verb.

1. Luisa y Daniela esperan **el autobús**.
    <u>*Luisa y Daniela **lo** esperan.*_____</u>
2. Veo <u>a María y Jorge.</u>
    _____

3. Miramos el vídeo.
_____

4. Hacemos la tarea.
_____

5. Adoramos los gatos y los perros.
_____

**F.** Re-write the sentences, converting the noun or proper noun to its corresponding <u>direct object pronoun</u>. In these examples, place the pronoun <u>before</u> the compound verb (*ir* + *'a'* + infinitive, present progressive).

1. Clara va a ver <u>a Ana Cristina</u> mañana por la tarde.
   __*Clara **la** va a ver mañana por la tarde.*_____
2. Estoy esperando <u>a Miguel</u>.
_____

3. Voy a comer <u>un burrito</u>.
_____

4. Estamos escuchando al profesor con mucha atención.
_____

**G.** Re-write the sentences, converting the noun or proper noun to its corresponding <u>direct object pronoun</u>. In these examples, place the pronoun <u>after</u> the compound verb (*ir* + *'a'* + infinitive, present progressive). Remember to add the accent.

1. Estoy buscando <u>las llaves</u>.
   _*Estoy buscándolas.*_____
2. Vamos a visitar <u>a los abuelos</u> en julio.
_____

3. Amalia está escribiendo <u>una novela</u>.
_____

4. Van a servir <u>la cena</u> a las ocho de la tarde.
_____

## "Double object" pronouns

Although not used in the song, one must know how to use the two pronouns when they are together in the same sentence or clause. There are two things to do:

1) Always place the *indirect object pronoun first*, immediately followed by the direct object pronoun, and
2) When the indirect object is in the third person (*le, les*) right before the direct object pronoun, the "le" and the "les" both must be converted instantly to "**se**" (no--never "ses"--"se" for both "le" and "les") before the direct object pronoun.

Ejemplo:
La madre siempre le lee <u>cuentos</u> **a su hija**.

The daughter becomes "se" before the "los":

La madre siempre **se** <u>los</u> lee.

Let's watch how a typical sentence in Spanish may be reduced to its bare essentials, reduced to the shortest possible utterance. (Even if you don't understand all of the grammar points omitted each time, you can still get the feel of it.)

**•El camarero les sirve café con leche a sus clientes.**
***The waiter serves coffee with milk to his customers.***
➔El camarero les sirve café con leche. (omits the indirect object)
➔Les sirve café con leche a sus clientes. (**or**, omits the subject)
➔Les sirve <u>café con leche</u>. (omits *both* subject and indirect object)
➔**Se** <u>lo</u> **sirve.** (transforms the direct object to its equivalent *pronoun* AND transforms the indirect object pronoun *Les* to *Se*, as explained above). In English: *He serves it to them.*

**•Ahora, Marta me da las noticias sobre la llegada de los bárbaros a las afueras de la ciudad.**
***Now Marta gives me the news about the arrival of the barbarians at the outskirts of the city.***
➔Marta me da las noticias sobre la llegada de los bárbaros a las afueras de la ciudad. (omits the adverb *Ahora*)
➔Marta me da <u>las noticias</u>. (omits the long adjectival phrase modifying *las noticias*)
➔Marta me <u>las</u> da. (transforms the direct object *las noticias* to the pronoun *las* and places it directly in front of the verb)
➔**Me las da.** (omits the subject *Marta*). In English: *She gives them to me.*

Note that one way of checking if you got it right, is to read the Spanish sentence *backward*, which in most cases will give you the direct English translation:

**Me** *las* <u>da</u> = <u>She gives</u> *them* to **me.**
**1**  *2* <u>3</u>     <u>3</u>     *2*   **1**

**H.** As in the above examples, reduce the following sentences to their essentials ("Se lo sirve," "Me las da," as in above)

1. Ana me va a dar una fiesta de cumpleaños en marzo.
   ___***Me la** va a dar.*_____
2. Óscar nos pide a nosotros un favor porque necesita ayuda.

   _____
3. Mi amigo me manda muchos *emails*.

   _____
4. Luis les va a tocar a los oyentes una canción de Albéniz.

   _____
5. Mi madre les va a preparar para ustedes una cena deliciosa.

   _____

## II. Stem-changing verbs *(sentir, mentir, querer, contar)*

Many verb conjugations in Spanish are *irregular*, that is, they do not end in the predictable six (6) forms as do the *regular* -AR, -ER, and -IR verbs. The good news is that although irregular, some classes of verbs are "regular in their irregularity." One such class of verbs is "stem changing," where the root vowel distorts into a dipthong (two vowel sounds joined together) in the "boot" section of the conjugation chart (when displayed with the singular on the left and the plural on the right--see below).

In this evolutionary distortion, the *-e-* becomes *-ie-* (querer—to want)

| qu**ie**ro | queremos |
|------------|----------|
| qu**ie**res | queréis |
| qu**ie**re | qu**ie**ren |

and the *-o-* becomes *-ue-* *(contar—to tell, to count)*:

| c**ue**nto | contamos |
|------------|----------|
| c**ue**ntas | contáis |
| c**ue**nta | c**ue**ntan |

Also included below is another type of stem-changing verb where the *-e-* simply changes to an *-i-* in the boot *(pedir--to ask for,* or *servir--to serve)*:

| p**i**do | pedimos |
|----------|---------|
| p**i**des | pedís |
| p**i**de | p**i**den |

**A.** Following this rule, please choose the appropriate verb infinitive from the list, and conjugate, so as to make the following sentences correct. The first one is done for you. Use each verb only once. Remember that you must conjugate these verbs, following the irregular patterns in the examples above. The vowel that changes is the vowel immediately preceding (before) the last syllable (in *despertar*, that would be the *second 'e'*, not the first). Also, the reflexive pronoun (*me, te, se,* etc.) where needed, is provided.

*despertarse (ie)*--to wake up   *encontrar (ue)*--to find   *poder (ue)* --to be able, can   *querer (ie)*--to want *sentir (ie)*--to feel  *mentir (ie)*--to lie  *volar (ue)*--to fly  *pedir (i)*--to ask for   *servir (i)*--to serve

1. (yo)_____*quiero*_____ comer muy bien esta noche. ¿Podemos ir a ese nuevo restaurante? Creo que se llama *"La Sevillana."*
2. ¿A qué hora (tú) te _____ los sábados?
3. Si no le (tú) _____ al camarero (waiter) nada, ¡no vamos a comer! Por favor, ¡decídete! porque yo tengo mucha hambre.
4. ¿(tú) _____ las vibraciones agresivas que vienen de ese hombre?
5. Esta bicicleta no _____ para nada. Está completamente oxidada (rusted).

6. (yo) _____ en avión cuando visito a mis abuelos.
7. ¿(usted) _____ venir ahora?  La niña está muy enferma.
8. Algunos líderes _____ con frecuencia, y otros dicen la verdad.
9. Siempre te (yo) _____ mirando la tele cuando llego a casa.

## III. *Siempre/Nunca (always/never)*

**A.** Write *siempre* or *nunca* in the blanks.

1. ___*Siempre*_____ me lavo las manos antes de comer.
2. _____ duermo más de quince horas.
3. _____ tomo un café por la mañana, todos los días.
4. _____ le pago al dependiente en el mercado cuando compro comida.
5. _____ digo con frecuencia que soy el rey de Canadá.
6. _____ escucho música mala.
7. _____ preparo la comida en el garaje.
8. _____ aprendo algo nuevo cada día.
9. _____ escucho a la profesora en la clase.
10. _____ me cepillo los dientes por la mañana.

## IV. *Contigo/Conmigo*

When using the preposition *con* ("with") in the first and second person singular ("with me," "with you"), you must use the irregular and unexpected *conmigo* and *contigo*, respectively (prepositional pronouns are covered in the song "*Nos Gusta*").

<u>*CON*</u> with <u>PREPOSITIONAL PRONOUNS</u>

| conmigo | con nosotros |
|---------|--------------|
| contigo | con vosotros |
| con él | con ellos |
| con ella | con ellas |
| con usted | con ustedes |

**A.** Translate to Spanish, using either *contigo* or *conmigo*:

1. She's going with you (ir)
   ___*Ella va contigo.*_____
2. Do you want to study with me? (estudiar)

   _____
3. I'll walk with you (use simple present tense, not future) (caminar)

   _____
4. Peace begins with me. (comenzar, ie)

   _____
5. She shares with me her ideas (compartir)

   _____

# V. *Gustaría, Sería, Quisiera*

These three verb forms are common, important, and advanced--and yet necessary to know at the beginning level:

*Me gustaría*--I would like
*Te gustaría*--you would like
*Le gustaría*--s/he or you (formal) would like
*Quisiera*--I would like
*Sería*--(it) would be

The forms that end in *-ía* are from the conditional verb tense (the "would" tense) and are not usually learned until the second or third level (high school *years* or college *semesters*). *Quisiera* is from the imperfect subjunctive tense (4th level) and for our present purposes should simply be memorized as "I would like…" It is the polite way to say "*Quiero…*" ("I want…").

**A.** Fill in the following with either *gustaría, sería*, or *quisiera*.

--_____ un café con leche, por favor.
--¿Te _____ tomarlo aquí, o para llevar?
--Para llevar, por favor. _____ también un sándwich de jamón.
--Vale. Un momento.
--¿Cuánto es?
--Ahhh, _____ cuatro y veinte euros.
--Gracias, señor.
--De nada, moza.

# VI. Possessive Pronouns

The possessive pronouns can be somewhat confusing at first. Here they are:

POSSESSIVE PRONOUNS

| Singular | Plural |
|---|---|
| mi(s)--my | nuestro(s)/nuestra(s)--our |
| tu(s)--your (familiar) | vuestro(s)/vuestra(s)--your (familiar) |
| su(s)--his/her/its/your (formal) | su(s)--their, your (formal) |

There are two main things to consider. The first is that when modifying plural nouns, the pronoun has to be plural also. Note:

mi casa--my house
mi**s** casa**s**--my house**s**

It would be like saying "my**s** house**s**" in English.

The second and more difficult thing to consider is the use of *su* and *sus*. In English, we are specific in the possessive ("his backpack," "her money," "their reasons," etc.). The only ambiguity in English is when you say "your house," because it could be the house of "you (two or more people)," or the house of an "you (the individual)"  And of course in English we don't have the *familiar* and *formal* differentiation of the use of *you* to worry about.

In Spanish, however, *su casa* could mean either *his house, her house, your (one person's) house, their house, and your (two or more persons') house*.  The solution to this problem is to *use the prepositional pronouns* in the third person singular and plural: *la casa de él, la casa de ella, la casa de usted, la casa de ellos/ellas, and la casa de ustedes*, respectively.  You can also use the nouns or proper nouns in the same construction, to clarify:  *la casa de Amalia, la casa del perro, etc.*  "Su" and "sus" are only used when it is already understood to whom one is referring.

CHART of POSSESSIVE PRONOUNS if using PREPOSITIONAL PRONOUNS for CLARIFICATION

| mi(s) casa(s)--my | nuestra(s) casa(s) <u>or</u> nuestro(s) coche(s) |
|---|---|
| tu(s) casa(s)--your | vuestra(s) casa(s) <u>or</u> vuestro(s) coche(s) |
| la(s) casa(s) de él | la(s) casa(s) de ellos |
| la(s) casa(s) de ella | la(s) casa(s) de ellas |
| la(s) casa(s) del perro (¡!) | la(s) casa(s) de los perros |
| la(s) casa(s) de usted | la(s) casa(s) de ustedes |

Finally, the beginning student often is confused when using *su* and *sus* because when talking about ownership and possession, there may be one or more owners, and there may be one or more things possessed.  This multiple duality can be confusing, and the student may wrongly use *sus* because there is more than one person doing the owning.  <u>The plural *sus* refers to the plurality of *things possessed*, not the plurality of owners.</u>

If the above seems confusing, it will all be clarified from the examples below.  Note them:

**su casa**--*his/her/its/your/their/your* (pl.) *house*.  There's only one house, so no matter how many people own it, you cannot put an 's' on that 'su'.

**su<u>s</u> casa<u>s</u>**--*his/her/its/your/their/your* (pl.) *house<u>s</u>*.  The 's' is added to both 'su' and 'casa' because there is now more than one house.  The number of owners remains the same.

Finally, note that with *nuestro/nuestr<u>a</u>* and *vuestr<u>o</u>/vuestr<u>a</u>* you must use the feminine form of the pronoun if the noun is feminine:

<u>Masculine noun:</u>   <u>Feminine noun:</u>
*nuestro amigo*   *nuestra amiga*

**A.** Write the correct possessive pronoun in the blank.

1. (Our) __*Nuestra*_____ casa es muy bonita.
2. (Your, familiar singular) _____ novio es simpático y guapo.
3. (Your, familiar plural) _____ exámenes (m.) están en mi casa.
4. (Their) _____ perro es muy pequeño.
5. (His) _____ hija asiste a la Universidad de California en Berkeley.
6. (Your, formal singular) _____ equipaje está en el taxi.
7. (Her) _____ maletas están en Miami.
8. (My) _____ problema es que no tengo dinero para pagar la luz.
9. (Our) _____ amigos siempre se reúnen aquí para ver la Copa Mundial.
10. Aquí está (your, formal singular) _____ café, señor.

**B.** Write the correct possessive pronoun in place of the prepositional pronouns.

1. Ésta es la casa de Bernarda Alba.
Ésta es ___*su*_____ casa.
2. ¿Son los libros de usted?
¿Son _____ libros?
3. Begoña es la novia de Jesús.
Es _____ novia.
4. Esos anteojos son de María.
Son _____ anteojos.
5. Este gobierno es de nosotros, los ciudadanos.
Es _____ gobierno.
6. El 22 de febrero es el cumpleaños de Clara.
El 22 de febrero es _____ cumpleaños.
7. Estas tierras son de ustedes.
Son _____ tierras.
8. El líder democrático no les quita los derechos constitucionales a los ciudadanos.
El líder democrático no les quita _____ derechos constitucionales.
9. Esta idea es de usted.
Esta es _____ idea.
10. La fiesta es la idea de Álvaro y yo.
La fiesta es _____ idea.

## 7. La Flor de Potosí

<u>Idiomatic expressions to learn before playing the song</u>:
*Potosí -- a city in south Bolivia once famous for its silver mines*
*valer un potosí -- to be worth one's weight in gold; to be worth a fortune*
*dime que sí -- tell me yes*
*lo cual -- which (erudite form)*

¡Qué_____! La Flor de Potosí
Dichoso día _____ yo te conocí
Ana María, dime tú que "sí",
que me quieres, _____ te quiero tanto a ti

Eres tierna, lo cual me gusta a mí
Eres _____ cuando sonríes así
Eres moza, y mozo soy, _____ ti
Eres dueña de mi_____, Potosí

En el otoño los dos nos conocimos
En el _____ nos enamoramos
En la primavera los dos nos prometemos
y en el _____nos casamos, ¡Potosí!

\_

En el otoño los dos nos conocimos
En el _____ nos enamoramos
En la primavera los dos nos prometemos
y en el _____nos casamos, ¡Potosí!

¡Qué_____! La Flor de Potosí
Dichoso día _____ yo te conocí
Ana María, dime tú que "sí",
Eres dueña de mi_____, Potosí
Eres dueña de mi_____, Potosí
Eres dueña de mi_____, Potosí
Eres dueña de mi_____, Potosí

Copyright Tom Blodget 2003

## El Banco de Palabras:
These are the words that are missing in the song:

cuando   invierno   linda   para   porque   alegría   verano   vida

# Vocabulario

Below are the words and phrases of the song in English, in the order of their appearance in the song. Fill in quickly as much of the Spanish as you know, without looking up any words in the dictionary or glossary. Any words or phrases that you *don't* know, which are "sandwiched" between words you *do* know, may be confidently identified by deduction. This method eliminates the need for a dictionary.

_____ what happiness!
_____ the Flower of Potosí
_____ lucky day
_____ when
_____ I met you
_____ Ana María, tell me that
_____ yes
_____ that you want me
_____ because I want you
_____ so much
_____ you
_____ You are tender
_____ which
_____ I like
_____ You are pretty
_____ when you smile
_____ like that
_____ You are a young lady
_____ and I am a young man
_____ for you
_____ You are the owner
_____ of my life, Potosí
_____ In the autumn/fall
_____ the two of us
_____ we met (each other)
_____ In the winter
_____ we fell in love
_____ In the spring
_____ we both are getting engaged
_____ and in the summer
_____ we shall be married, Potosí!
…(repeats)

## Preguntas Orales.

These questions are to check for comprehension, and should be asked orally after listening to the song several times with the above activities.

1. ¿Son jóvenes o viejos?

2. ¿Cómo se llama la moza, la joven?

3. "La Flor de Potosí" se refiere al hombre o a la mujer?

4. ¿Cuánto tiempo va a pasar entre el momento en que se conocieron, y cuando se van a casar? ¿una semana? ¿un mes? ¿nueve meses? ¿cinco años?

5. ¿Está feliz o triste el hombre?

6. ¿En qué estación se van a casar? ¿en el otoño? ¿en la primavera? ¿en el invierno? ¿en el verano?

7. ¿Es simpática o antipática Ana María, según el que canta?

8. Mi estación favorita es _____ . ¿Cuál es tu estación favorita?

## I. *Las Cuatro Estaciones*

**A.** Write in the season in the blanks, based on the information. For these examples, you need not use the *el* or *la*.

(la) primavera    (el) verano    (el) otoño    (el) invierno

1. Las plantas crecen y florecen en *primavera* .
2. Si nieva, nieva en _____ .
3. Se llevan abrigos de lana, botas, y guantes de cuero en _____ .
4. Tenemos vacaciones en _____
5. La gente juega en la playa, nada en el mar, y toma el sol en _____ .
6. Hace mucho frío en _____
7. Hace mucho calor en _____ .
8. Se dice que hace mucho viento en _____, pero la verdad es que *se nota* más el viento porque la evidencia de su acción se ve en la caída de las hojas de los árboles. Durante las otras estaciones, las hojas no caen, aunque hace viento también.
9. Mucha gente tiene alergias y ellos tienen que limpiar el moco de la nariz y las lágrimas de los ojos en _____ .
10. Las vacaciones de la Navidad son en _____ .
11. Cuando es verano en la Canadá, es _____ en la Argentina.
12. La estación cuando las flores emiten su perfume es _____ .
13. Se practica el esquí en _____ .
14. La cosecha de los tomates es en _____ .

15. La cosecha de la lechuga es en _____.
16. La cosecha de las calabazas es en _____.
17. La cosecha de las naranjas es en _____.
18. Hay más agua fluyendo en los ríos y las montañas en _____.
19. Octubre es en _____.
20. El Día de los Muertos y el Día de Todos los Santos se celebra en

_____.
21. Se celebra el Día del Año Nuevo en _____.
22. Se celebra la Pascua en _____.
23. Se celebra el día de la Independencia de los Estados Unidos en _____.
24. En Nueva York, nieva más en _____.
25. En Hawaii, "siempre es _____."

# II. Reciprocal Reflexive Verbs

The reciprocal reflexives conjugate the same way as the reflexives (see "*¿Me quedo o me voy?*"), and only in the plural (in the singular they are simply reflexive actions that one does to oneself, not two or more people doing something to each other).

| |
|---|
| Nos miramos—We look at each other |
| Os miráis—You guys look at each other |
| Se Miran—They look at each other |
| You look at each other |

Conocerse—to meet or to know each other
Enamorarse—to fall in love (with each other)*
Prometerse—to get engaged (to each other)*
Casarse—to get married (to each other)*
Frecuentarse—too see each other frequently, to hang out together
Amarse—to love one another/each other
Mirarse—to look at each other (with *fijadamente* it means "to stare at each other")
Ayudarse—to help each other
Matarse—to kill each other
Llevarse bien (con)—to get along well with each other

*the parentheses indicate that the verb is also simply reflexive and not necessarily reciprocal. *Me enamoro (*from *enamorarse) de ella* translates as *I fell in love with her.* She may or may not have fallen in love with him, however (not necessarily reciprocal therefore).

**A.** Conjugate the 10 verbs above in the ten blanks below. Use each verb only once, and choose the **best** answer for each.

1. Romeo y Julieta __*se enamoran*__ a pesar de los conflictos entre sus familias.
2. Si las personas trabajando juntos en una oficina no __*se llevan bien*__, hay mucho estrés, la compañía sufre, y nadie lo pasa muy bien.
3. Jaime es gran amigo. Hace mucho tiempo que nosotros _____.

4. En varios lugares geográficos del mundo, hay grupos o naciones que
_____ en guerras como resultado de disputas sobre la tierra, la religión,
la injusticia, o el poder político.

5. Antes de *(infinitive form here:)*_____ , muchos enamorados

(6.)_____ , y la mujer lleva un anillo que significa esa promesa y ese amor.

7. Cuando van al restaurante, los novios _____ fijadamente por mucho
tiempo sin comer.

8. --Si ustedes _____ uno a otro con todo su corazón, y si ustedes tienen
mucha paciencia, les aseguro que pronto ustedes van a experimentar una paz más allá de su
comprensión actual.

9. Nosotros tenemos que *(infinitive form with"nos":)*_____ si queremos
vivir en comunidad, en paz, en armonía.  Es decir, tenemos que compartir y sacrificarnos por los
demás.  La comunidad no puede existir, ni puede sobrevivir, si cada persona sólo piensa en sí.

10.  Los padres de Ana notan que Ana y Emilio--un joven que tiene 25 años (Ana tiene 16)--
_____ mucho, en casa o en la calle.  Los padres se preocupan mucho
porque creen que su hija es demasiada joven, y no debe salir con un hombre de esa edad.


# III. *Ser* with descriptive adjectives

(see also the *ser/estar* contrast in "¿Me quedo o me voy?")

When describing someone, or some thing, the verb *ser* is used:

SER—to be

| | |
|---|---|
| *Soy*—I am | *Somos*—we are |
| *Eres*—you are | *Sois*—you are |
| *Es*—s/he, it is, you are | *Son*—they are, you are |

Descriptive adjectives, as all adjectives, have to agree in gender with the noun they modify:

*Ese hombre es guap**o**.*
*Esa mujer es guap**a**.*

And in number:

*Eso**s** hombr**es** son guapo**s**.*
*Esa**s** mujer**es** son guapa**s**.*

**A.** Below is a list of useful adjectives for people, followed by some exercises.  Choose the best
answer to complete the sentence.  The adjectives are given in their singular *feminine* or neuter
form (textbooks always use the masculine as a default position; I'd like to be different this time.
In any case, it's the same challenge, but this time the boys will have to work harder).  You may
have to make them plural or masculine, or any combination that is called for.

Note also that some of the adjectives that describe a person's weight, lack of attractiveness, and even height would certainly be considered *rude* in English speaking countries ("you're skinny"). I dare say that in some Spanish speaking countries people can be a bit more frank ("Eres flaco, hombre"), and you're not supposed to get all sensitive about it. I personally disagree, but must report what I witnessed and felt (having been "flaco" at the time!). Certainly in Spain people speak more bluntly, more directly to your face.

guapa—handsome or good-looking
hermosa—dreamily gorgeous, beautiful
bonita—cute, pretty
linda—beautiful, pretty, cute
fea—ugly
alta—tall
baja—short
flaca—skinny
gorda—fat
fuerte—strong
débil—weak
simpática—nice
antipática—mean
joven—young
vieja—old
pobre—poor
rica—rich
inteligente/lista—intelligent/smart
estúpida/tonta—stupid/dumb
feliz/contenta—happy, content
triste—sad
cómica—funny
graciosa—witty, funny
aburrida—boring
aburridísima—really really boring
interesante—interesting
intelectual—intellectual
humilde—humble
arrogante--arrogant
rara—strange (literally "rare"; reserved for people you don't want to hang out with at all because they behave unpredictably and stifle opportunities for a good time, usually because of an emotional or mental eccentricity. To be considered "rara" is one of the worst things imaginable, socially. But of course, if you are *rara*, you may not know it, because it's reserved for gossip rather than constructive criticism; people just avoid you when they can, and tolerate you when they must).
norteamericana—(what citizens of the U.S. mean when they say "American");
europea—European
africana—African
latinoaméricana—Latin American
asiática—Asian
india—native American, or Indian from India

1. La persona se siente muy __*feliz*_____ el día en que gana la lotería.
2. Para jugar al básquetbol, es útil ser _____.
3. Para montar a caballo en las carreras y llegar primero a la línea de llegada (*finish line*), es necesario ser _____.
4. Las mujeres que son actrices casi siempre son _____.
5. Los hombres que son actores no tienen que ser muy _____.
6. La mayoría de los esclavos (los que trabajan sin ser pagados, los que no tienen la libertad ni derechos civiles) en los últimos quinientos (500) años tienen antepasados (*ancestors*) _____.
7. Las personas _____ pueden competir en los deportes al nivel profesional.
8. La persona que habla mal de los demás (others), y que engaña (deceives) y roba y miente es _____.
9. La persona que tiene 96 años ha vivido mucho tiempo; es _____.
10. La persona que siempre piensa en la injusticia, la falta de compasión, y la violencia que hay en el mundo puede ser una persona _____ a veces. También, esa conciencia de la realidad a veces le hace a la persona más simpática, inteligente, y humilde.

**B.** Below is a list of useful adjectives for things, followed by some exercises.

nueva—new
usada—used
limpia—clean
sucia—dirty
útil—useful
inútil—useless
barata—inexpensive
cara—expensive
difícil—difficult
fácil—easy

1. La cocina del restaurante no está sucia, está _*limpia*_____.
2. Acabo de comprar mi coche ayer. Tiene solamente 17 kilómetros. Es _____.
3. Aprender el español en dos meses es _____.
4. Una computadora sin electricidad es completamente _____.
5. Es más barato comprar ropa _____.

**C.** LOS COLORES. Although there were no colors in the song, colors are used with the verb *ser* when describing the usual color of things. Fill in the colors below. Remember thay have to agree in gender (**la** cas**a** blanc**a**) and in number (la**s** nube**s** gris**es**).

blanca—white
negra—black
gris—grey
amarilla-yellow
azul—blue

roja—red
verde—green
anaranjada—orange
morada—purple
rosada—pink
marrón/café—brown

1. Cuando el sol sale, y el cielo está completamente nublado, el cielo está _gris____ .
2. Cuando el sol sale (y no hay nubes) el cielo está _____ .
3. Cuando el sol se pone, y salen las estrellas (pero no la luna), y es medianoche, el cielo está

_____ .
4. Las bananas son _____ .
5. En las guerras, La Cruz _____ lleva a los heridos (injured) al hospital.
6. El presidente de los Estados Unidos vive en la Casa _____ .
7. El presidente de la Argentina vive en la Casa _____ .
8. Los que sufren heridos en la guerra reciben la Medalla del Corazón _____ .
9. La naranja es _____ .
10. El color de la tierra, y de la carne cocinada, es _____ .

**CHORDS to the songs**. It is hoped that those who play the guitar or piano or other instrument, and like the songs, will find these chord sequences adequate for figuring out how to play the songs for your own enjoyment.

**La Luz del Sol.** Key Am. INTRO: Lead in Am (no chord)/Am Em C Em Am / Em D E7 Am/ Am Em C C D / Em D Am (2x) / VOCALS: CHORUS: Am, AmGAm / CDEm / AmGAm / Am / VERSE: Am G Am G / Am G Am Am / Am G Am G / Am G Am Am / INSTR BREAK: same as chords in intro. VERSE: repeats above. LEAD BREAK: Am G EmGAm / Am G Am/ Am G EmGAm / Am G Am/ Em D Am / Em D E7 Am /Em D Am / G Am / G Am/ CHORUS: repeats. VERSE: repeats OUTRO: Am G Am G / Am G Am Am / Am G Am G / Am G Am Am / (outro repeats four times). ENDING same as intro but add Em D Am / Em G Am…/ at end.

**¿Me Quedo o Me Voy?.** Key Em. VERSE 1: Em D Em Em / Em D Em Em / Em D D C / G D C Em  VERSE 2: repeat above but add D C Em / D C Em  INSTRUMENTAL LEAD repeats verse 2, but add at end another D C Em / Em… VERSE 3: same as instrumental, ends on Em for 2 bars, then to E.

**La Fiesta.** Key Am. VERSE 1: Am D Am / Am C Am G Am / Am D Am / Am C Am G Am / D Am / D Am / D Am /Em  G/Am  VERSE 2: repeats. CHORUS: D D / Am Am / D D / Am Am. VERSE 3, INSTRUMENTAL, and VERSE 4 all repeat.  Add 4 bars of Am at end of song.

**Nos Gusta.** Key D. INTRO VOCALS: A G / D A / A G / D A / F C / G G / Bb F / G G / Bb F / G G  VERSE 1/VERSE 2: DAGD DAGD  BREAK: A G / A G  VERSE 3/ INSTRUMENTAL: repeats.  BREAK repeats.  VERSE 4 repeats.  OUTRO VOCALS same as INTRO VOCALS.

**Amañamo.** Key Em. INTRO Em on 7$^{th}$ and 9$^{th}$ frets. VERSE: Em Em Em Bm (4x). CHORUS: C D D G / Em Am GCG / C D D G / G Em G Em G Em D Em… Verse and chorus are same throughout.  Instrumental same as verse.

**Te Quiero Como Eres.** Key Em. INTRO: G D C G C G D…. (2x). VERSE 1: G Em (4x), then C G C G C G D D; G Em G Em G Em C D C D C D G Em Am D7, G Em Am D7. INSTRUMENTAL: G Em G Em C D C D C D, G Em Am D7, G Em Am D7. VERSE 2 repeats.  OUTRO G Em (8x).

**La Flor de Potosí.** Key C#m. (Bass GB) C#m B G#m / C#m B B / C#m B G#m / B A C#m. BRIDGE: G#m B6 (bar 4$^{th}$ fret DGBE strings) A / G#m B6 A / G#m B6 A / B A C#m. OUTRO add B A C#m three more times.

# ANSWER KEY

## 1. La Luz del Sol
**Preguntas Orales**: 1. por la mañana 2. mucho 3. vegetales 4. bien; no 5. mala calidad 6. feliz 7. en el centro de la luz 8. dentro.  **I.A:** 1. quiero 2. despiertas 3. pides 4. sientes 5. sirve 6. vuelo 7. puede 8. mienten 9. encuentro  **II.A:** 1. gustan 2. importan 3. parece 4. queda 5. falta  **IIIA:** 1. el agua 2. el águila 3. el alma 4. el alba  **IV.A:** (en orden): día, amanece, alba, noche, luz, sol, campo, pueblo, cultivamos, vegetales, cosechamos, pedriza, alma, belleza  **V.A:** 1. charity 2. novelty.  **V.B:** 1. verity 2. culpability 3. infirmity 4. amity  **V.C:** 1. mocedad 2. ciudad 3. voluntad 4. edad 5. bondad 6. mitad 7. soledad

## 2. ¿Me Quedo o Me Voy?
**Preguntas Orales:** 1. sí 2. no 3. Cantinflas 4. mucho 5. sí 6. no 7. posiblemente/tal vez 8. No, porque le tormenta/la sonrisa es falsa 9. irse, no  **I.A:** 1. location 2. condition  **I.B:** 1. es 2. son 3. es 4. está 5. es 6. es 7. está, es 8. es 9. son 10. es  **II.A:** 1. voy, estoy 2. soy 3. Estoy 4. doy 5. voy 6. Soy 7. Estoy 8. doy 9. Soy 10. Estoy  **III.A:** 1. Nos 2. Le 3. Te 4. Les 5. Les 6. Me 7. Le 8. Te 9. Le 10. Os  **IV.A:** 1. estoy enojado 2. estoy confundido 3. estoy ocupado 4. estoy cansado 5. estoy enamorado 6. estoy enloquecido 7. estoy casada 8. estoy aburrida 9. estoy entusiasmada 10. estoy decepcionada 11. estoy distraída 12. estoy liberada  **V.A:** 1. hipertensión 2. división 3. opresión 4. decisión 5. invasión 6. compasión 7. confusión 8. impresión 9. obsesión 10. precisión  **V.B:** 1. excepción 2. distribución 3. constitución 4. atención 5. destrucción 6. construcción 7. emoción 8. satisfacción 9. polución 10. pronunciación 11. investigación  **VI.A:** 1. madurez 2. rigidez 3. niñez 4. vejez 5. aridez 6. estupidez  **VII.A:** 1. me cepillo 2. me acuesto 3. me peino 4. me preparo 5. me pongo 6. me lavo 7. me ducho 8. me quito 9. me afeito 10. me levanto

## 3. La Fiesta
**Preguntas Orales:** 1. sábado 2. cumpleaños 3. mucha 4. mucha 5. al supermercado 6. no; sí 7. todo tipo de bebidas 8. muchas personas 9. bailar; cantar 10. una ensalada 11. cerca de la casa 12. patatas ali oli, mejillones, tortillas españolas 13. la mujer 14. no 15. la mujer  **I.A:** 1b 2b 3c 4c 5c 6c 7c 8c 9b 10b 11b 12c 13c 14b 15c 16c 17c 18b 19c 20c 21c 22c 23c 24c  **I.B:** 1R 2CO 3BA 4CA 5CA 6F 7CA 8P 9CA 10CO 11BA 12R 13V 14BA 15V 16V 17M 18CO 19CO 20CO 21F 22V 23M 24 F or V  **II.A:** 1J 2K 3H 4E 5B 6A 7I 8L 9F 10N 11C 12G 13D 14M  **III.A:** *Cerca:* 1. este 2. esta 3 estas 4. esta 5. estos 6. esta 7. este 8. estos 9. este 10 este  *Lejos:* 1. esas 2. esas 3. esa 4. esos 5. ese 6. esa 7. ese 8. esa 9. esos 10. esa  **IV.A:** Tengo que hacerlo. 2. Hay que hacerlo. 3. Tenemos que ir ahora. 4. Tiene(s/n) que trabajar hoy? 5. Hay que leer este libro.  **V.A:** (en orden) 53467218  **V.B:** (en orden) 17,14,9,12,10,16,11,15,13,18  **V.C:** (en orden) 15,4,14,9,6,13,10,8,12,7  **VI.A:** bailando, cantando, tomando, comiendo  **VI.B:** bailar, cantar, tomar, comer

## 4. Nos Gusta
**Preguntas Orales** 1. el bienestar, comida, comunidad, y un buen hogar 2. sí; sí; sí 3. sí 4. es atlética 5. el campo 6. las vacas 7. a las dos 8. sí 9. *answers vary* 10. *answers vary*  **I.A:** 1. Me gusta comer 2. Me gusta el perro, Átlas. 3. Me gusta la escuela. 4. Me gusta cantar. 5. Me gusta mi nuevo coche.  **I.B:** 1. Me gustan los libros. 2. Me gustan las fotos. 3. Me gustan Ana y Luisa. 4. Me gustan las manzanas. 5. Me gustan los profesores.  **I.C:** A ustedes siempre les gusta ganar el partido  **I.D:** 1. Le 2. Nos 3. Le 4. Le 5. Te 6. Os 7. Me 8. Le 9. Les 10. Les  **I.E:** 1. vivir en paz 2. el agua 3. estudiar 4. esperar por mucho tiempo 5. correr 6. cantar 7. dormir en el salón 8. la paella 9. La Copa del Mundo 10. visitar con los nietos  **I.F:** (en orden) DFIHJGAECB  **I.G:** answers vary  **II.A:** 1. también 2. tampoco 3. también 4. también 5. también 6. tampoco  **III.A:** 1. La 2. la 3. los 4. el 5. la 6. las 7. el 8. la; la 9. los; las 10. las 11. la; el; la; la

12. Las **III.B:** 1. el arroz 2. reloj 3. el mar 4. la clase 5. el hombre 6. la mujer 7. la paz 8. la red 9. el coche 10. el olor 11. la ley 12. el tren 13. el papel 14. el estrés 15. el bienestar 16. el país 17. la luz **IV.A:** 1. sabón 2. corazón 3. campeón 4. razón 5. jamón 6. ladrón 7. limón 8. melón 9. barrigón 10. montón **V.A:** 1. criar animales; tomar el aire 2. nos gusta almorzar; estar en casa

## 5. Amañamo

**Preguntas Orales:** 1. no; no; sí 2. sí 3. Tal vez; sí 4. Tal vez **I.A:** 1. hago 2. traigo 3. salgo 4. oigo 5. digo 6. pongo 7. veo 8. hago 9. oigo 10. salgo **II.A:** 1. sé (6) 2. conozco (1) 3. conozco (3) 4. sé (7) 5. conozco (3) 6. conozco (1) 7. conozco (2) **III.A:** 1. deben 2. quiere 3. Puedo 4. podemos 5. puedo 6. Debo 7. Debes 8. Queréis 9. puedo 10. quiero **IV.A:** 1. con 2. con 3. sin 4. sin 5. con **V.A:** 1. Estoy comiéndome el coco. 2. Me estás haciendo un gran favor. 3. Te estoy esperando aquí. 4. No estoy entendiéndote. 5. Estás volviéndome loco.

## 6. Te quiero como eres

**Preguntas Orales:** 1. Le gusta tal como es. 2. es una idea de él 3. sí 4. siempre se frecuentan 5. extrovertido 6. sí; no 7. guapa **I.A:** 1. Le doy mi amor 2. Le dicen (cuentan) las noticias. 3. Les sirvo la ensalada. 4. Les preparamos la comida. 5. Me cantáis canciones bonitas. **I.B:** 1. No la saben. 2. La ve. 3. Lo lava. 4. La como. 5. La tomamos. **I.C:** 1. nos 2. me 3. les 4. les 5. te **I.D:** 1. le 2. te 3. le 4. os 5. les **I.E:** Luisa y Daniela lo esperan. 2. Los veo 3. Lo miramos. 4. La hacemos 5. Los adoramos. **I.F:** 1. Clara la va a ver mañana por la tarde. 2. Lo estoy esperando. 3. Lo voy a comer. 4. Lo estamos escuchando... **I.G:** 1. Estoy buscándolas. 2. Vamos a visitarlos. 3. Amalia está escribiéndola. 4. Van a servirla. **I.H:** 1. Me la va a dar. 2. Nos lo pide (favor=lo). 3. Me los manda (emails=los). 4. Se la va a tocar/Va a tocársela (una canción=la). 5. Se la va a preparar/Va a preparársela (una cena=la). **II.A.** 1. siempre 2. nunca 3. siempre 4. siempre 5. nunca 6. nunca 7. nunca 8. siempre 9.siempre 10. siempre **III.A:** 1. Ella va contigo. 2. ¿Quieres estudiar conmigo? 3. Camino contigo 4. La paz comienza conmigo mismo. 5. Ella comparte conmigo sus ideas. **IV.A:** Quisiera; gustaría; Quisiera; sería. **V.A:** 1. Nuestra 2. Tu 3. Vuestros 4. Su 5. Su 6. Su 7. Sus 8. Mi 9. Nuestros 10. su **V.B:** 1. su 2. sus 3. su 4. sus 5. nuestro 6. su 7. sus 8. nuestros _or_ sus (_point of view_) 9. su 10. nuestra (note that _nuestra, f.,_ refers to the _idea, f._)

## 7. La Flor de Potosí

**Preguntas Orales:** 1. jóvenes 2. Ana María 3. la mujer 4. nueve meses 5. feliz 6. verano 7. simpática 8. _answer varies_ **I.A:** 1. primavera 2. invierno 3. invierno 4. verano 5. verano 6. invierno 7. verano 8. otoño 9. primavera 10. invierno 11. invierno 12. primavera 13. invierno 14. verano 15. invierno (depends) 16. otoño 17. verano 18. primavera (snowmelt) 19. otoño 20. otoño 21. invierno 22. primavera 23. verano 24. invierno 25. primavera **II.A:** 1. se enamoran 2. se llevan bien 3. nos conocemos 4. se matan 5. casarse 6. se prometen 7. se miran 8. se aman 9. ayudarnos 10. se frecuentan **III.A:** 1. feliz 2. alta/o 3. bajo/a 4. bonitas, etc. 5. guapos 6. africanos 7. fuertes 8. antipática 9. vieja 10. triste **III.B:** 1. limpia 2. nuevo 3. difícil 4. inútil 5. usada **III.C:** 1. gris 2. azul 3. negra 4. amarillas 5. Roja 6. Blanca 7. Rosada 8. morado 9. anaranjada 10. marrón/café

_If you find any of these answers or assertions about grammar, etc., <u>incorrect</u> or debatable, please email me at blodget @ snowcrest . net and with any other comments you have about this book or CD. Thanks!_

_Tom Blodget_